W9-BOE-112

A Winterthur Series Book

The symbol of the Winterthur Series, shown on the preceding page, is a detail from "America Guided by Wisdom," engraved by Benjamin Tanner after John J. Barrelet, Philadelphia, *circa* 1810.

GRANDEUR on the APPOQUINIMINK

The Corbit House, entrance hall

GRANDEUR on the APPOQUINIMINK

THE HOUSE OF WILLIAM CORBIT AT ODESSA, DELAWARE

JOHN A. H. SWEENEY

UNIVERSITY OF DELAWARE PRESS

1959

Library of Congress Catalog Card Number: 59-7532

Manufactured in the United States of America by the Quinn & Boden Company, Inc., Rahway, N. J.

To

Mrs. Francis B. Crowninshield

whose respect for our heritage has inspired

countless Americans to work toward

its preservation

Preface

Grandeur on the Appoquinimink is the first volume in the Winterthur Series, to be published by the University of Delaware Press. The Winterthur Program in Early American Culture, offered by the University in cooperation with The Henry Francis du Pont Winterthur Museum, was established in 1952 with the support of the Rockefeller and Avalon Foundations.

The goal of this unique program of cooperation between a great museum and its university neighbor is to promote the broadest possible understanding among the people of our nation through an integrated study of America's early culture, including its European origins and formative years. Courses in English and American history, art, literature, and thought are given on the campus of the University. These courses are coordinated with laboratory work at the Museum. In the latter, distinctive instruction in curatorial practice and in connoisseurship is also given. In addition, the master's thesis is an important requirement. It affords the graduate student an opportunity to make an original contribution to a relatively unexplored field of study.

The course of study embodies three key principles in its approach to the arts. First, the arts cannot be understood in terms of "pure form." Architecture, town planning, and the design of utilitarian objects, such as furniture and pottery, are man's solution to the problems of daily living, and, therefore, the objects themselves become fully intelligible only when studied in relation to those problems. Furthermore, representational painting and sculpture can be fully understood only if one considers their iconography and symbolism as well as their forms. Since the problems created and solved, and the iconography and symbolism employed, are culturally determined, art must be studied within the framework of culture.

Secondly, a study of the American arts must give equal treatment to the major and the so-called "minor" arts. Art forms of the "professional artist" represent only a small area in the total aesthetic expression of any culture, and frequently are atypical of the art as a whole. Further, the main stream of development in the art of the United States to 1840 was influenced in direction by the work of craftsmen rather than by that of artists and professional architects. Such craft forms as furniture, ceramics, glass, silver and pewter objects, carpentry, masonry, and textiles make the art of those early days in America understandable.

Thirdly, a study of the arts and of the role of the artist and artisan in society yields data not only of aesthetic importance but also of significance to social history. Artifacts, buildings, and sites connected with life in earlier times are vital aspects of history as well as of art. Special emphasis is placed therefore on laboratory work with art objects, both in museums and in the field.

The Winterthur studies completed thus far have emphasized the arts in America prior to 1840. They have been based largely on primary sources, both as to objects and documents. This study by Mr. John A. H. Sweeney, Associate Curator of the Winterthur Museum, is the first to appear in print, and appropriately so. Mr. Sweeney was an outstanding student in the first graduating class of Winterthur fellows. His subject is of importance to those interested in early American architecture and American decorative arts. It is hoped that the publication of *Grandeur on the Appoquinimink* and of the other studies that will follow in the Winterthur Series will make an important contribution to an understanding of American culture.

JOHN A. PERKINS
President
University of Delaware

Contents

PAGE

PREFACE ix

FOREWORD xiii

CHAPTER

I The Place 3

II The Man 13

III The House 39

IV The Record 69

V The Epilogue 75

APPENDICES

A. William Corbit's Building Accounts 81

B. Bill of Robert May & Company 86

C. Deed for the Corbit House Site 94

D. Will of William Corbit 96

E. Minutes for the Will of Mary Cowgill Corbit 100

F. Division of William Corbit's Furniture 101

G. Inventory of William Corbit's Estate 102

H. William Corbit's Library 106

I. William Corbit's Furniture 110

J. Genealogical Chart 125

BIBLIOGRAPHY 131

INDEX 139

Illustrations

PAGE

The Corbit House, entrance hall iv
The Corbit House, entrance front 2
The Corbit House, *circa* 1870 7
The Corbit House, office or pantry 12
Marriage Certificate of William Corbit and Mary Pennell . . 21
Survey of the Corbit Property, 1777 38
The Corbit House, parlor 40
The Corbit House, plan of first and second floors 41
The Corbit House Drawing Room 51
The Powel House Drawing Room 51
Detail of cornice molding, Powel House Drawing Room . . 53
Detail of chair-rail molding, Corbit House Drawing Room . . 53
Detail of base molding, Corbit House Drawing Room . . . 53
Detail, Swan's *Designs in Architecture*, Plate 32 54
Detail, Swan's *Designs in Architecture*, Plate 40 54
Swan's *Designs in Architecture*, Plate 23 55
The David Wilson House, Odessa, Delaware 58
The John Lewden House, Christiana, Delaware 59
The James Moore House, near Odessa, Delaware 59
Bill from Robert May & Co., 1774 68
Old Drawyers Church, near Odessa, Delaware 74
Existing Furniture of William Corbit 120

The photograph of the drawing room of the Powel House is reproduced herein through the courtesy of the Philadelphia Museum of Art; all other photographic illustrations are the work of Gilbert Ask.

Foreword

The Corbit House at Odessa is a monument in the history of Delaware. Standing near the point where the King's Highway crossed the Appoquinimink Creek, this house reflects the prosperity of the commercial town that grew up around the junction of two routes of travel. It serves as a reminder of the time when the "Lower Counties," which later became the State of Delaware, were thriving as a center of American wheat production. It recalls, too, a community oriented toward the water, for this part of New Castle County was economically and socially connected with Philadelphia by means of the Appoquinimink Creek and the Delaware River.

The house itself is an important example of American-Georgian architecture, well known for its fine woodwork and related in form and plan to important Philadelphia houses of the period. It also stands as a reminder and a reflection of its builder, William Corbit—tanner, farmer, and land speculator. A successful businessman and a leader in the community, Corbit may be considered a typical eighteenth-century man. Born on January 21, 1746, he was above all a practical man; yet he appears to have been educated and sociable, for the inventory of his estate indicates good taste and his library shows an unusual breadth of interests. His business activities reflect an American pattern of investing in real estate; he applied the profits of his tannery toward the creation of more wealth by purchasing farm land in Delaware and city lots in Philadelphia.

William Corbit's house and the existing documents concerning it form the artifacts which reveal the story of his life and the lives of his neighbors. An account of the cost of building his house, the carpenter's bill, and the inventory of Corbit's estate are only a few of the most important of scores of papers which pertain to this man and his family. Through such documents light is cast on the society of the times, and through them that society can be reconstructed. In this book the Corbit House is presented as a reflection of its builder and his life, bringing together facts which reveal a small but vital part of the pattern of American culture.

I am indebted to all those who have taken an interest in this project and have been of help to me in the preparation of the manuscript. In particular I wish to express my appreciation to Mr. H. Rodney Sharp for permission to make this study and for sharing the knowledge gained from his careful and sympathetic restoration of the Corbit House, and also to Mrs. Charles Lee Reese, Jr., great-great-granddaughter of William Corbit, who has constantly encouraged me and has graciously provided me with family history and documents. Special thanks for their generous co-operation are due other descendants of William Corbit: Mrs. Earle R. Crowe, Mr. A. Burtis Hallock, Mr. Anthony Higgins, Mrs. Albert W. Morse, Jr., Mrs. Paul J. Nowland, Mrs. Samuel F. Pryor III, Mrs. D. Meredith Reese, and Mrs. William C. Spruance. I am further indebted to Miss Helen R. Belknap, Miss M. Elinor Betts, Miss Gertrude Brincklé, Mr. Thomas E. Burrough, Mr. Leon de Valinger, Jr., Miss Jeannette Eckman, Mrs. Howard Greene, Mr. George F. Kelly, Miss Louise Le Patourel, Mrs. Louis Moeller, Mr. Charles F. Montgomery, Dr. Ernest J. Moyne, Dr. John A. Munroe, Dr. Frank H. Sommer III, Mr. David H. Stockwell, Miss Marion E. Wilson, and the staffs of the Friends Historical Library, the Historical Society of Delaware, the Historical Society of Pennsylvania, the Memorial Library of the University of Delaware, and the Public Archives Commission of the State of Delaware.

To my family I am grateful for their patience and encouragement, and to the Winterthur Committee of the University of Delaware I am especially indebted for undertaking the publishing of this book as one in the Winterthur Series.

JOHN A. H. SWEENEY

Wilmington, Delaware
April, 1959

GRANDEUR on the APPOQUINIMINK

The Corbit House, entrance front

Chapter 1

The Place

In the spring of 1775 Robert Honyman, a Scottish doctor traveling from Virginia to Rhode Island, noted in his journal his impressions of lower New Castle County and nearby Maryland: "The Country still pretty open & well cultivated, fine large, level fields of Wheat, & here & there divided with skirts of woods, tall, stout timber. On this side of the Bay one sees none of the grand Palaces that are so frequent in Maryland on the other side, but the houses are of a more inferior sort, much more numerous, neat enough, & the fields round them. the stock & every thing else in good order, & the people themselves look well & hearty." [1] The descendants of many of these people continue to farm the large level fields, and the general appearance of the countryside is much as it was described on the eve of the Revolutionary War, except that concrete highways now follow the route taken by Dr. Honyman and connect the villages which grew up to serve the eighteenth-century farmers.

Situated amid these prosperous Delaware farm lands, 22 miles south of Wilmington, is the town of Odessa. Originally called Appoquinimink —sometimes Appoquinimink Bridge—and later Cantwell's Bridge, it is now known to motorists only as a crossroads on the Du Pont Parkway. Yet in and around Odessa are preserved some of the outstanding examples of eighteenth-century Delaware architecture. On a slope overlooking the northern approach to the village is Old Drawyers Presbyterian Church, and not far away stands the brick Friends Meeting House; the public library is housed in the handsome David Wilson Mansion, home of one of the town's early merchants.

At the eastern end of the tree-shaded main street of Odessa stands the Corbit House, foremost of the town's Georgian buildings and considered one of the outstanding buildings of its type in the Delaware Valley. Ivy covers the solid north wall facing the street, while the east, or entrance, front of the house commands a sweeping view across green meadows to the Appoquinimink Creek, where William Corbit, the builder of the house, established his tannery in 1767.[2] The tannery is gone; ships no longer ply the once-busy Appoquinimink; and from its vantage point the Corbit House, like the town, quietly contemplates its past.

The land upon which Odessa is located was granted originally to Alexander de Hinijossa, a Dutchman and the director of the settlement at New Amstel.[3] The earliest reference to the area was made by Jasper Danckaerts, an agent for a group of Dutch Labadists, who went through Appoquinimink in 1679 on his way to Bohemia Manor and described the settlement as a small village situated on a creek. He commented on the hospitality of the inhabitants: "They are all Dutch who live here. . . . We stepped into a house and were welcome. Some food was immediately set before us to eat, and among other things butter, cheese, and rye bread which was fresh and so delicious that my companion said it was to him like sweet cake." [4] De Hinijossa had planned to retire to Appoquinimink and engage in the fur trade when he finished his official duties in 1663, but he had owned the land only a few months when the colony was taken over by the English and his grant confiscated.

Into this Dutch settlement then came an Englishman. In 1676 Sir Edmund Andros, Governor of New York, granted a large tract of land on the Appoquinimink to Captain Edmund Cantwell, who was high sheriff on the Delaware under Andros and later sheriff of New Castle County under the new proprietor, William Penn.[5] Cantwell added to his holdings until, at the time of his death in 1698, he controlled more than 4,000 acres and was considered one of the important landowners in the lower part of the county.[6] In 1731 Cantwell's son Richard, a justice of the peace, to whom he had willed his "lower plantation," was given authority by the General Court to erect a toll bridge across the Creek and to take a half acre of land at fair valuation from Abraham Martin, who lived nearby, as the site of the toll house.[7] Although there had been a settlement here as early as the 1670's and the area was sufficiently populated by Presbyterians for them to build a meetinghouse in 1711, the bridge now provided the stimulus for the growth of a commercial village.

The Appoquinimink, like the other streams that twist their way from the center of the peninsula through the marshes into the Delaware River or Bay, provided high land sites that could be developed as small ports, safe from storms and pirates. At the bridge the Creek curves around a hill, forming a sort of promontory; here storehouses were built and wharves constructed. To this landing, shallow-draft vessels made their way up the Appoquinimink, thus establishing a link between the inland farms and the broader avenue of transportation, the river. Being only a few miles from the deep-water points on the Bohemia and Sassafras Rivers, Appoquinimink Bridge, as it was first known, became an important stop on one of the routes between the Chesapeake Bay and Philadelphia. "Herman's cart-road," connecting Bohemia Manor in Cecil County with the Appoquinimink, had been laid out as early as 1660.[8] Danckaerts described this as a broad cart road, eight miles long, over which "the goods which go from the South [Delaware] River to Maryland by land, are carried, and also those which pass inland from Maryland to the South River." [9]

This path was supplemented in 1762, when a branch of the King's Highway leading from Wilmington via Christiana and Red Lion to Dover crossed the little bridge.[10] The more direct route used by travelers from Philadelphia to Annapolis led from Christiana to Head of Elk or from Red Lion through Middletown to the Sassafras River; and therefore it would seem that the traffic to Appoquinimink was composed of local farmers using the landing and storehouses. Over these trails came wagons loaded with wheat, corn, oats, and barley to be transferred to the shallops at the wharf and carried down the Creek to the Delaware and thence to Philadelphia. At this time the wheat of the peninsula possessed "an uncommon softness and whiteness, very favourable to the manufacture of superfine flour," and was prized by colonial millers and in foreign markets as well.[11] At least a part of the wealth of the Brandywine millers and the Philadelphia merchants who traded extensively with the West Indies was thus channeled through the rising port on the Appoquinimink. By the 1760's David Wilson, an enterprising young man from Sussex County, had opened a general store on the hill above the landing.[12]

Bridge, wharf, and store were the factors which brought economic importance to the Appoquinimink. There can be no doubt that the surrounding country was good farm land. William Guthrie wrote in 1795 that "the soil along the Delaware river, and from eight to ten miles into the interior country, is generally a rich clay, producing large timber, and well adapted to the various purposes of agriculture." [13] The entries in David Wilson's ledger attest to the extent of this area influenced by the trading center; in addition to dozens of farmers who traded with Wilson from Appoquinimink Hundred across the Creek to the south and from St. Georges Hundred on the north, there were many from settlements in the neighboring province of Maryland—Bohemia Manor, Head of Chester, Warwick, Sassafras, and even as far away as Queen Anne's County. Appoquinimink, or Cantwell's Bridge, as it gradually came to be known after the middle of the century, can be considered typical of the grain centers which dotted the peninsula—Christiana Bridge, Newport, Duck Creek, and Little Creek, to name a few.

Records of the trade at Cantwell's Bridge are not available, but the shipments from Duck Creek, 12 miles away, are indicative. Seventy-five thousand bushels of wheat, 50,000 bushels of corn, 2,000 bushels of oats, 8,000 bushels of barley, 3,000 barrels of flaxseed, 1,000 barrels of pork, and 20,000 staves sent abroad annually from Duck Creek provide adequate proof of the agricultural prosperity of this region in the years preceding the Revolution.[14] Guthrie summed up the economic life of the village twenty years later: "The principal business is the transportation of flour and grain to Philadelphia and Brandywine, and the sale of foreign goods for the consumption of the neighbourhood." [15]

If the bridge and the wharf drew to Appoquinimink farmers and merchants from all over the county, the trading activity of the village brought its inhabitants into contact with Philadelphia and the world beyond. The accounts of ship captains and storekeepers prove that the city was the source of imported foods and consumer goods. Travel to

The Corbit House (*circa* 1870), from an old photograph in the possession of Mrs. Charles Lee Reese, Jr.

Philadelphia by shallop was convenient, if not entirely elegant, and the round trip could be made in two days.[16] William Corbit, when writing to his son who was apprenticed to a tanner in Philadelphia, referred constantly to "going up to town," apparently attaching no more importance to the distance than does the modern commuter. Only once did he indicate that such trips might be "fateaguing." [17]

While commerce was the primary reason for this travel, there was much activity of a purely social nature. Diaries and letters reveal the constant visiting and traveling up and down the peninsula. By 1794 a stage went through Appoquinimink twice a week on its way from Dover to Wilmington; and this trip, which could be made in a single day, undoubtedly contributed to increased visiting.[18] It was not unusual for Philadelphians to have family connections in the Lower Counties, and many owned property there as well. Sharp Delany, the cultured collector of customs for the Port of Philadelphia, came into possession of real estate at Appoquinimink through his marriage to Margaret Robinson, who actually lived at Naaman's but was heiress to land at Appoquinimink.[19] Because they were under the jurisdiction of the Philadelphia Yearly Meeting of Friends, Quakers living in the vicinity of Appoquinimink looked to the city for their religious direction, a fact that also had social and cultural implications for their community. To attend the quarterly and yearly meetings, they, together with other Quakers from within a hundred-mile radius of Philadelphia, poured into the city, where they attended to church business, visited friends and relatives, and brought themselves up to date on the news since their previous trips.

The influence which Philadelphia exerted over the surrounding parts of rural Pennsylvania, New Jersey, and Delaware was continuously reinforced by ties such as these; and it is therefore not surprising that the economic and social patterns of life in the Lower Counties should resemble those of the city. The close business and social contacts, the visits and intermarriages of Philadelphians and Delawareans make the term *Philadelawarean* an apt one.[20] It is a term which might well be applied to William Corbit. His mother was a member of a prominent Pennsylvania family; he was born on his grandfather's farm in Chester County, grew up at Appoquinimink, but went to Philadelphia to learn his trade. Later, when he had established his tannery on the Appoquinimink, he sold his products and bought furniture in the city, eventually acquired land there, and traveled back and forth frequently between his properties.

With a life divided between country and city, it is not unusual to find that William Corbit's tastes reflected his contacts in Delaware and Philadelphia—a fact evident in his house, his furniture, his letters, and his books. Appoquinimink was certainly simpler than Philadelphia, and Corbit's life can be considered a simpler version of the lives of the merchants with whom he traded in Philadelphia. His house, accordingly, was a simpler version of the country mansions these men were building on the banks of the Schuylkill, and the plan and many of the architectural details of the Corbit House relate it closely to Philadelphia town houses. In a man's house is mirrored the man himself; and in the Corbit House is to be found not only the story of William Corbit, but that of his community and of the entire scope of his activities. The house, then, serves as a summary of the relationship of the country town of Appoquinimink to the metropolis fifty miles to the north.

Notes to Chapter 1

1. Robert Honyman, *Colonial Panorama, 1775; Dr. Robert Honyman's Journal for March and April*, Philip Padelford, ed. (San Marino, California, 1939), p. 10.

2. Genealogical Society of Pennsylvania, "Copy of Records (1705-1800) of Duck Creek Monthly Meeting of Friends," I, 305 (June 27, 1767). Hereafter cited as Duck Creek MM.

3. J. Thomas Scharf, *History of Delaware 1609-1888* (Philadelphia, 1888), p. 1005.

4. Jasper Danckaerts, *Journal of Jasper Danckaerts 1679-1680*, Bartlett Burleigh James and J. Franklin Jameson, eds. (New York, 1952), p. 130.

5. Scharf, *loc. cit.*

6. A MS patent, dated 1676, from Governor Andros to Cantwell for 800 acres bounded by the Appoquinimink Creek was in the possession of the Corbit family until 1954, when it was presented to the Public Archives Commission of the State of Delaware.

7. George Foot, *An Address, Embracing the Early History of Delaware, and the Settlement of Its Boundaries, and of the Drawyers Congregation . . .* (Philadelphia, 1842), p. 14.

8. Scharf, *op. cit.*, p. 991.

9. Danckaerts, *op. cit.*, p. 127.

10. Scharf, *loc. cit.*

11. William Guthrie, *A New System of Modern Geography* (Philadelphia, 1795), II, 457.

12. David Wilson Mansion, Inc., "Ledger, 1766-1771."

13. Guthrie, *loc. cit.*

14. John A. Munroe, "The Eve of the Revolution," *Delaware, a History of the First State*, H. Clay Reed, ed. (New York, 1947), I, 84-85.

15. Guthrie, *op. cit.*, II, 460.

16. John A. Munroe, *Federalist Delaware 1775-1815* (New Brunswick, New Jersey, 1954), p. 33.

17. Historical Society of Delaware, Corbit-Higgins-Spruance Papers, Fol. 4, William Corbit to Pennell Corbit, Appoquinimink, October 20, 1796. Hereafter cited as Corbit-Higgins-Spruance Papers.

18. Munroe, *loc. cit.*, p. 139.

19. Margaret Robinson was the daughter of Thomas Robinson, of Naaman's Creek, who owned a large tract of land at Appoquinimink which originally may have included the land upon which the Corbit House was built. (New Castle County Deeds, Book Z, Fol. 274.) Delany served as executor of his mother-in-law's estate in 1791. (National Society of Colonial Dames of America in the State of Delaware, *A Calendar of Delaware Wills, New Castle County 1682-1800* [New York, 1911], p. 123.)

20. John A. Munroe, "The Philadelawareans: a Study in the Relations Between Philadelphia and Delaware in the Late Eighteenth Century," *Pennsylvania Magazine of History and Biography*, LXIX (April, 1945), 128-49. See also John A. H. Sweeney, "The Norris-Fisher Correspondence: A Circle of Friends, 1779-82," *Delaware History*, VI (March, 1955), 187-232.

The Corbit House, office or pantry

Chapter 2

The Man

Although he was born in Chester County and learned his trade in Philadelphia, William Corbit belonged to the farm lands of lower New Castle County. It is known that his grandfather, Daniel Corbit, referred to in family genealogies as a Scotsman, was living in the vicinity of Appoquinimink as early as 1717, when his name appears in the records of Duck Creek Monthly Meeting as one of the witnesses at the marriage of John Macoole and Mary Howie.[1] Thereafter, he was mentioned repeatedly in the minutes of the meeting as the representative from Georges Creek Preparative Meeting, which was located near Port Penn and was attended by the Corbits until 1783, when the meeting was transferred to Cantwell's Bridge.

In 1723 Daniel Corbit acquired a farm of 250 acres on the south side of the Appoquinimink Creek and two years later purchased a still larger tract from John Grant for the sum of £190. This second farm, half marsh and half upland, was part of the grant originally patented to Robert Moreton by Governor Francis Lovelace in 1671 and described by Scharf as "betwixt Blackbird Creek and Appaquimime: Bounded on ye east wth appaquimimy creek: on ye south with a branch wch extendeth it self westerly out of the same creek . . . and on ye opposite two sides with ye Maine Woods." [2]

Here, on the cleared land between the forest and the water, Daniel Corbit lived for thirty years with his large family. At his death in 1756 he willed his plantation to his son Daniel, entailing the larger part of it to his grandson Daniel and a second tract known as "Middle Neck" to his grandson Israel Corbit.[3] The inventory filed with this will indicates that Corbit was a man of some means. In addition to a large quantity of furniture, including eighteen chairs, four beds, and seven chests, the inventory lists eighteen forks and eleven knives, fifty-three pounds of pewter, and enough farm equipment to indicate that the Corbit farm was a comfortable and self-sufficient establishment.[4] This "moveable estate" was divided among Corbit's daughter Rachel Duhadaway and his grandchildren John McCool and Rachel Lewden.[5]

Daniel Corbit's first wife is recorded in the family Bible as Elizabeth Holdt. No more is known about her, although it is possible that the spelling of her name is a corruption of Hoodt, for the Brinton genealogy refers to one Casper Hoodt's mentioning his "daughter Elizabeth, wife of Daniel Corbett of New Castle County" in his will, dated 1732.[6] In any event the first Mrs. Corbit can be presumed dead by 1732, for in March of 1729 Daniel Corbit had announced before the Duck Creek Monthly Meeting that he intended to marry Mary Humphries.[7] Later that year the administration papers of Caleb Offley's estate listed Daniel Corbit as co-executor with "Elizabeth his wife late Widdow & Execx. of Caleb Offley dec'd."[8] It would appear, therefore, that Daniel Corbit had married, instead of Mary Humphries, Mrs. Elizabeth England Offley, who brought with her to the farm on the Appoquinimink three young sons by her previous marriage, Michael, Caleb, and David, each of whom had inherited tracts of farm land in New Castle County from his father.[9]

Through his activity as a Quaker and through this second marriage it is evident that the prosperous yeoman Daniel Corbit had close contacts with other farm families of the region. His daughters by his first wife married local farmers. In the summer of 1737 Ruth Corbit was married to Samuel McCool; and in 1743, at a ceremony in her father's house witnessed by Corbits, Offleys, and various in-laws, Rachel Corbit became the wife of Jacob Duhadaway.[10] The third Corbit daughter, Mary, married Josiah Lewden of Newport.[11]

Daniel Corbit II, born October 11, 1715, left the family farm in 1739 and went to Chester County, Pennsylvania, where, on November 8 of that year, at the meeting house in Birmingham, he was married to Mary

Brinton, the daughter of William and Jane Brinton.[12] While this was the first recorded marriage of the Brintons and the Corbits, it was perhaps not the first time the two families had come into contact. The *Brinton-Corbit Book* points out that there were Corbets in Shropshire, where they were closely connected with the Brintons as early as the thirteenth century; and, while no relationship with the Corbit family in America is defined in this genealogy, it is perhaps significant that when the first William Brinton emigrated in 1683 his certificate of transfer to the Philadelphia Yearly Meeting of Friends was signed by a William Corbet.[13]

The Brinton holdings in Birmingham and Thornbury Townships stretched from Brinton's Mill at Concord westward to the Brandywine, comprising at various times more than a thousand acres. Somewhere on this rolling farm land, which is still dotted with the solid stone houses built by various members of the Brinton clan, Daniel and Mary settled down; and here their six children were born. The exact location of their house is unknown, but it was presumably close to the elder Brintons' homestead, now restored and open to the public as the 1704 House. The two-room cottage used by the Brintons' other daughter, Ann, and her husband, Samuel Bettle, was a half mile away and stood until recently, when it was torn down for the widening of Route 202.

Daniel Corbit apparently farmed some of his father-in-law's acres until 1752, when, shortly after the death of William Brinton, he returned with his family to Appoquinimink.[14] Four years later, he inherited his father's plantation and also his clothes, consisting of "one suit with Cote, Vest and Breeches and Shirt." [15] He was now a freeholder in his own right and a man of some substance, with possibly a broader outlook on life because of his residence among the prosperous Quaker farmers and millers of Pennsylvania. How well he had been accepted by the Brintons and their Chester County relatives is not documented; but, for an unexplained reason, William Brinton established a trust of £300, the interest on which was to be paid to Mary Corbit after the death of her parents. Should she be widowed, the principal and interest were to be paid to her in three yearly installments, but until that time it was not to be the property of her husband; at her death the principal was to be divided among her children.[16] Mary Corbit inherited no further property from her father, but at her mother's death she and her sister were joint heirs to her furniture and personal estate.[17] Daniel Corbit and Samuel Bettle signed the receipt for this legacy.[18] Although the Bettles moved to Philadelphia in 1749 and the Corbits did not return to Birmingham except for an occasional visit, the relationship of the families continued to be an intimate one for more than half a century.

In Delaware, Daniel Corbit, like his father, was a leader of the community, although he occasionally deviated from the accepted behavior of a Quaker gentleman. The Friends of Georges Creek Meeting complained against him for "keeping Loose and Vain Company and drinking Strong Liquor to excess and when overtaken therewith frequent using of vain unsavory Expression." [19] When he died in 1774, he left the respectable estate of £260 in cash, two plantations on the Appoquinimink entailed to his first and second sons, and two lots in Wilmington and a lot on the south side of Christina Creek which he directed to be sold.[20] Daniel's death ended the second generation of the Corbit family in America. His had also been the second generation on the Appoquinimink farm. His stewardship had been good, for he had been able to invest in speculative real estate; and, while his father had left only land and personal property, Daniel was able to leave a substantial amount of cash to his heirs. His children, however, had already begun to extend the scope of their activity beyond this waterside farm; and within two generations, with the family scattered as far as Philadelphia, the farms would no longer be in their possession.

It would appear that the increased wealth in the Corbit family, a fact which paralleled the growth of Cantwell's Bridge and the increasing communication with Philadelphia, was the cause of a gradual breakdown in the local orientation of the family's activities. Two of Daniel Corbit's sons married sisters from Wilmington; a third married a woman from Salem, New Jersey. A further breakdown in the family unity is seen in the fact that the sons all married "out of meeting," and Corbit's daughter became the wife of David Wilson, who was not a Quaker.[21]

Daniel Corbit III and his brother Israel, the two oldest sons, with their futures secure as the heirs to the family farms, remained on the land; but William Corbit, the third living son, had to learn a trade in order to support himself. Accordingly, in 1765, in the spring of his twentieth year, William Corbit went to Philadelphia to learn the tanner's trade, carrying with him a certificate of transfer to the Philadelphia Monthly Meeting.[22] There he spent two years under the instruction of his cousin William Bettle before he returned to Cantwell's Bridge.[23]

Corbit had perhaps had some training in a trade before he went to Philadelphia, for the length of time he spent there was considerably shorter than the normal apprenticeship of seven years. Since there is no earlier record of his transfer to another monthly meeting, it is possible that he had been apprenticed to a tanner in New Castle County and later, at the rather advanced age of twenty, went to Philadelphia. His relationship with his master was probably a cordial one, for William Bettle was only eleven years older than Corbit and was also his first cousin, the son of Samuel and Ann Brinton Bettle, who had moved to Philadelphia from Chester County in 1749. Bettle, married to Sarah Beakes of Trenton, operated his tannery on the northern outskirts of Philadelphia and, in addition, owned a small farm 3 miles from town.[24] When Bettle died, five years after William Corbit left his employ, his widow advertised the business for sale; and the description in the *Pennsylvania Chronicle* provides a picture of the tannery in which Corbit presumably received his training:

> A Large and commodious Tanyard, in the Northern-Liberties, near this City, on the south side of a certain lane called Long-Lane, between Third and Fourth-streets continued. The Lot contains in breadth, east and west, on the said lane, one hundred feet, and in length or depth, north and south, two hundred feet; bounded on the north by said lane on the east by Edmund Woolly's ground; on the south by a certain run of water called Pegg's Run. The Tanyard consists of thirty-seven vats, twelve handlers, three limes and three bates. There is on the premises a bark-house, large enough to contain two hundred cords of bark, and every other building necessary and convenient for a complete Tanyard, all in good order; also a well of good water, with a new pump in it, at the head

> of the yard; likewise a new well built stable and chair house, with a loft over the whole for hay. The whole subject to a ground-rent of Forty-six Spanish Dollars and two thirds of a Dollar per annum.[25]

The location was perhaps the leather district, for a later advertisement points out that Bettle's tanyard was between those of Samuel Noble and George Schlosser.[26] A contemporary writer on commerce remarked that tanning was a business which provided a good return on the investment, and Bettle's affluence is perhaps indicated by the fact that he had the time and interest to take out a membership in the Library Company of Philadelphia.[27] Corbit's two-year stay with the Bettles undoubtedly had an effect on his own interests.

When he came back to the country in the summer of 1767, William Corbit was presumably a self-confident young man, for he was master of a trade and had already become acquainted with people from many places. The first seven years of his life had been spent in Birmingham Township and the next thirteen on the farm near Cantwell's Bridge, where it had been possible for him to meet the farmers, merchants, and tradesmen who came to this little commercial center from the whole of the Eastern Shore as well as from Philadelphia. He had lived the last two years in the city, where he had observed urban habits and had acquired urban tastes, as his house was later to prove. With a keen eye for business, young William Corbit decided to establish a tannery a few hundred feet upstream from the toll bridge. Two factors probably prompted him in his decision: the obvious need for leather in the bustling village and the availability of good Spanish-oak bark, an essential ingredient in the process of tanning.[28] Where Corbit raised the necessary capital is not known; he apparently only leased the land he used for a tanyard, for he bought no property until 1771.[29]

Quercus falcata, or Spanish oak, was native to southern New Castle County; thus William Corbit was in a better position than the Philadelphia tanners, who used the columns of the *Pennsylvania Gazette* to beg the Delaware farmers to ship oak bark to them.[30] A good supply of animal skins was also available in the country, and Corbit's account with his neighbor David Wilson shows hides to be the largest single item he purchased.[31] From his later correspondence it is evident that Corbit often purchased hides in Philadelphia as well, shipping them to Appoquinimink to be processed and returned to the city for sale. Another factor important to the location of a tannery was a supply of running water for the washing of hides, and of this there was plenty in the Creek. A large amount of land was not necessary to the tanning operation, as is indicated by the fact that William Bettle's tanyard, where Corbit learned his trade, was less than half an acre. However, a variety of equipment was needed; Bishop points this out by including among the "rude appointments" of a tannery "a number of oblong boxes or hogsheads sunk in the earth near a small stream, and without cover or outlet below, to serve as vats and leeches, a few similar boxes above ground for lime vats and pools, an open shed for a beam house, and a circular trough fifteen feet in diameter, in which the bark was crushed by alternate wooden and stone wheels, turned by two old or blind horses at the rate of half a cord a day . . ."[32]

The process of tanning followed by William Corbit was that of replacing the gelatinous substance in the fibers of hides and skins with tannin (an astringent in oak bark), thus rendering the hide durable and impermeable to water. To achieve this, the hides were first washed, then periodically immersed in lime pits for as long as eighteen months in order to soften them. At this point any residual hair and flesh were scraped off and the hides then stretched horizontally in a tan pit, each hide covered with a powder of ground tanbark, and the pit filled with water. After soaking here for four months or more, depending upon the thickness of the hides, they were removed, dried, stretched, and taken to a currying shop to be finished.[33]

William Corbit carried on this work with the help of a journeyman and an occasional laborer, as mentioned in his letters.[34] He apparently ground his own bark, for he noted in another letter that he had purchased a mill horse.[35] While tanning and currying were separate trades, a tanner often performed both operations; Corbit had a currying shop in his tanyard, and it is assumed that he finished his leather there.[36] With such an operation William Corbit was able to keep his capital investment relatively small, to process the hides and sell them for cash, which would enable him to increase his working capital and to invest his profits in real estate. As late as 1832, when Corbit's son Daniel was operating the tannery, the capital investment of $2,000 was equal to only one-third of the stock and cash on hand, and the annual product of the tannery was placed at $3,850. At that time the tannery employed two men (who worked for $16 a month) and made use of nine horses.[37] Some English tanners realized as much as a 40 per cent return on their investment; whether William Corbit was as fortunate is not known, but the prosperity of his tannery became evident soon after its establishment.

Shortly after his return to Cantwell's Bridge, William Corbit married Elizabeth Empson, daughter of a local family. No record of the marriage is found in the Corbit Papers, and the only specific reference to Elizabeth Empson Corbit is an entry in the minutes of Duck Creek Monthly Meeting:

> The Women Friends request our Assistance in drawing a testimony against Elizabeth Empson (that was) now the wife of William Corbitt for accomplishing her marriage with him by the assistance of a priest. . . .[38]

No other reference to Elizabeth Empson has been found, but the name of her family appeared in the records at Duck Creek as early as 1693, when Cornelius Empson, a justice of the peace, married Sarah Wilson. At the time of the testimony against Elizabeth Corbit, David Wilson, the other promising businessman at the Bridge, was married to Margaret Empson, who was the daughter of Cornelius and Mary Empson and who may have been the sister of Elizabeth. Margaret Empson Wilson died in 1768, and after her death Wilson took as his second wife William Corbit's sister Mary.[39] The careers of these two men were to cross again and again throughout the next fifty years.

There are indications that the independence and energy displayed by William Corbit in his business affairs were matched by an equally strong independence in his personal life. When the Friends of Georges Creek complained that he had bought a Negro slave, contrary to the directions of the Philadelphia Yearly Meeting, Corbit steadfastly refused to free the

New Castle County ss } These are to Certify to whome it may Concern that William Corbit & mary Pennell Both of the County aforsaid were Duly Published agreable to act of assembley by me one of his majestys Justices of the Peace for New Castle County

John Jones

These are further to Certify that I william Corbit of the County afors.d took mary Pennell to be my Lawfull wedded wife in the Presence of John Jones Esquire & the rest of the Subscribers agreable to an act of assembley of the County of New Castle Kent & Sussex upon Delaware I mary Pennell of the County afors.d Do like william Corbit to be my Lawfull wedded husband in the Presence of the above mentioned Justice of the Peace & the rest of the Subscribers agreable to an act of assembley as above mentioned as witness our hands 19th Febry 1773

John Jones

Wm Corbit

Mary Corbit

Rachel Sharp

Hannah Delany

Mary Wilson

Sarah her mark Britton

David Wilson

Mat. Delany

John Kille

Joshua Boone

Robt. May

Joseph Hanson

John Swayne

Ann Griffith

Marriage Certificate of William Corbit and Mary Pennell, from the original document in the Corbit Papers

man. The case dragged on for seven months, and Corbit, "not in a disposition likely to make satisfaction," was disowned by the Monthly Meeting.[40] Relations with his family were obviously strained, for his father, while leaving large bequests to his other children, cut William out of his will in 1774.[41] Perhaps the unrecorded marriage to Elizabeth Empson was the cause of the breach, or perhaps it was due to an immoderate amount of worldliness on William's part, as evidenced in the splendid mansion which he had begun to build near his tannery in 1772. Perhaps another reason was a second marriage, also "out of meeting," to Mary Pennell, of Wilmington, on February 19, 1773.[42]

It might have been said of Mary Pennell, as it was of her contemporary, Polly Norris, of Fairhill, that "she was a young lady endowed with every qualification requisite to make the marriage state happy."[43] Twenty-three years old, educated, and possessed of nearly £700 in her own right, she had lived near Appoquinimink for a year while her stepfather, Jonas Preston, operated a mill on Drawyers Creek.[44] Born at Upper Providence in Chester County in 1749, she was the daughter of Thomas and Mary Yarnall Pennell.[45] Her father, who apparently had been a merchant-miller owning 116 acres on Ridley Creek and a house and lot in Chester, died intestate before his daughter was a year old. He left an estate valued at £2,404, of which Mary inherited a one-fifth share.[46] Mary Pennell's mother had married three times, with an apparent preference for millers. Her second marriage took place in 1752 to John Lea, whose son established the Lea mills on the Brandywine; her third marriage was to Jonas Preston, presumably of Chester for the family moved from there to Appoquinimink in 1769.[47] Jonas Preston died early in the winter of 1773, a fact which might help to explain the unusual circumstances of the Corbit-Pennell marriage.[48] The ceremony was performed by John Jones, Esquire, a justice of the peace, and also a miller and large landholder in St. Georges and Appoquinimink Hundreds. Twelve persons signed the certificate; and of this group only two, David and Mary Corbit Wilson, were related to the bride and groom.[49]

The fine house that William Corbit was building would not be ready for more than a year; and by that time the family was to be increased by a son, Thomas, born in November, 1774. Two years later, another son, Pennell, was born; in 1779, Edward; and in 1781, a second Thomas. Mary Pennell Corbit died on June 8, 1783, at the age of thirty-three.[50] No family records of this marriage have survived, and any description of the life of the Corbits must be inferred from legal documents. The year 1774 was apparently one of grief, for William Corbit's father, mother, his brother, and presumably his son, died within twelve months.[51] Although he had been disowned by his father, William Corbit nonetheless received a sixth share of the trust established for his mother by his grandfather Brinton. That he was not estranged from the entire family is indicated by the fact that he was acting as guardian for the children of his deceased brother John when the principal of this trust fund was divided.[52]

During these years, from 1773 until her death in 1783, Mary Pennell Corbit watched her husband prosper in business and invest the profits in farm land across the Creek in Appoquinimink Hundred; in 1775 he had bought 37 acres between the Creek and the King's Road from James and Prudence Moore.[53] In March, 1777, he had given Joseph Alexander £500 as the first payment toward the purchase of a 200-acre farm already seeded with wheat, and by August of that year the entire debt of £1,400 had been paid.[54] By 1783 the Corbits had purchased 300 more acres of marsh, meadow, and woodland.[55] The farm land provided grain and other agricultural products, and the woodland was a likely source of tanbark.

There is no indication that the Corbits suffered from the war which embroiled the country and which, in September, 1777, had come close to the farms of their cousins in Chester County. A family tradition, quoted in Scharf's *History of Delaware*, claims that Continental soldiers once came to the tannery to buy leather. When William Corbit, opposed to war even though a disowned Quaker, refused to sell, the soldiers searched first the tanyard and then the house, where they found piles of leather stored in the cellar. Taking the goods, they left Continental money in payment, but the notes were never redeemed and were said by Scharf to be in the possession of William Corbit's grandson in 1888.[56] Whether the story is fact or fiction is not clear, since no notes now exist. At any rate, William Corbit, vouched for by Edward Martin, went before

William Allfree on July 18, 1778, and "swore or affirmed" his allegiance to the State of Delaware and held himself not bound to the King.[57] If this seems contradictory to Quaker principles, it must be remembered that William Corbit was not a member of the Society of Friends in 1778.

Although Mary Pennell Corbit had "gone out in Marriage," she had remained an active Friend. Shortly after her marriage she transferred her membership from the Wilmington Monthly Meeting to Duck Creek.[58] On November 24, 1781, perhaps at his wife's persuasion, William Corbit appeared at the Monthly Meeting with a "Paper of Acknowledgement and Condemnation of conduct" for marriage by the assistance of a magistrate and for purchasing a Negro as a slave. He freed the slave and paid him for his service.[59] By June of 1784, Corbit was clerk of the Monthly Meeting, and was prominent in Quaker affairs for the rest of his life.[60]

Less than two years after his wife's death, William Corbit married again. This time he chose Sarah Fisher, of Duck Creek, the daughter of Fenwick Fisher, a merchant, and Mary Holliday Fisher. They announced their intentions of marriage on November 27, 1784; and, William Corbit being found free of other marriage engagements, they were married on December 29.[61] Sally Fisher Corbit was more than a belle of Duck Creek, for, while she had many suitors among the country squires, she had often visited her Fisher cousins in Philadelphia and was a favorite with the Quaker bachelors there. She was a close friend of Deborah Norris Logan, the young mistress of Stenton, who was considered the most brilliant hostess in Philadelphia.[62] Little is recorded of the life of William and Sarah Corbit; but, through her, William Corbit must have been drawn into closer communication with Philadelphia. He had kept up his association with that city through his business contacts; now, with his wife's cousins there, and her friends among such important Quaker families as the Logans, the Dickinsons, and the Norrises, he had many social contacts as well. In an undated letter, Mrs. John Dickinson told Sarah Corbit that William had been at Meeting (presumably in Philadelphia) and that she was expecting him to call.[63] In the city on business, William Corbit faithfully attended Meeting and found time to visit the Dickinsons, who owned farms in Kent County and with whom he would have had much in common.

The marriage of William Corbit and Sarah Fisher lasted only five years, but three children were born to them: two daughters who died in infancy and a son, William Fisher Corbit, born on January 18, 1789. Sarah Fisher Corbit died at the age of thirty-one, five weeks after the birth of her son.[64]

Again a widower, and now left with three small children, William Corbit turned to their nurse, Mrs. Alice Murry, to hold his family together. "Alcy," as the Corbit children called her, remained with the Corbits for more than thirty years. She was regarded as a member of the family, and the state of her health was included as an item of importance in almost every letter. When he drew up his will, Corbit designated this loyal servant a "beloved and kind ancient friend," and he ordered his children to provide her with an annuity of $50 a year.[65] When she died five months later at the age of seventy-one, Corbit entered her death date in the family Bible with those of his wives and children.

William Corbit married a fourth time. On April 28, 1791, at a crowded ceremony in the Little Creek Friends Meeting House in Kent County, he took as his new wife thirty-year-old Mary Cowgill, the daughter of John Cowgill, large landholder and leader of the Friends, known as "the Quaker Martyr" for his sufferings during the Revolution.[66] This marriage was long and happy, and Mary Corbit survived her husband by twenty-eight years. Six children were born of the union: John Cowgill (1792-1832), Sarah (1795-1860), Daniel (1796-1877), Mary (1798-1826), Thomas (1803-1820), and Rachel Thomas (1808).[67] Daniel Corbit, named for his grandfather, survived all his brothers and sisters and followed his father as tanner, landholder, and squire of Cantwell's Bridge.

In the spring of 1792 Corbit history began to repeat itself: Pennell, the eldest of William Corbit's sons, was sent to Philadelphia to learn the tanning trade and to acquire an education.[68] William Corbit followed his son's progress with care, sending him money for clothes "of middling quality" and books for the improvement of his mind, as well as words of encouragement regarding his study of French and geography.[69] The letters were addressed to Pennell in care of Thomas Scattergood, who was listed in the *Philadelphia Directory* for 1791 as a tanner living at 278 North Front Street and who was probably Pennell's master. These letters reveal William Corbit's attitude toward the value of education and show him to have been a practical man in this respect as well as in business. Writing to Pennell at the outset of the boy's apprenticeship, he suggested: ". . . I recommend thy Industry and attention to business, in order to gain the good will of thy Master and Mistress, who I flatter My Self will not require more of thee than is right and reasonable." [70] Corbit was also aware of the importance of academic training to a businessman, for on May 8, 1790, he had written:

> . . . I have it much at Heart that thee Should be Enable by a Tollarable Share of Plain education, to become quallified to transact the verious occurrances of life that may fall under thy notice with propriety, and now seems to me the time for thee to lay the foundation for useful improvement. . . .
>
> . . . One thing more I wish thee to acquaint thy self with, and that is the meaning of common words made use of in books thee reads and writing Letters, which is essentially necessery. Perhaps it will be necessery to provide thyself with a Dictionery for that purpos—not that I wish thee to make use of high flown words unnessesserely, that is pedantick, but learn by degrees the meaning of words particularly those that are made use of in common conversation, in order to form a good stile in writing which is considered as an accomplishment as well as advantage in the common occurrances of life. . . .
>
> I repeat it again, pay every attention to thy Learning, that the expence tharein may be amply paide in thy improvement, which will afford full sattisfaction to me for all charges accrewing nscecerely for that purpos.[71]

Another letter indicates that William Corbit himself was well read and regarded books as a vicarious means of studying life:

> Agreeable to thy request I have sent by Dan[l] Richards one Vollum of Extracts from different authers, Selected for the improvment of youth—as well as others, I hope thee will be able to discriminate between the

> most valluable part and that of the least improving, as most authors has more or less of both containd in their works when they are large and volumnious, There is two more I shall send thee after has read this through and hope thee will improve therefrom. as writings of Men of Reflection and observation has a great tendency to improve the mind of youth as well as those of more advance years, hope thee will Select the most useful part containd in the vollum I now send and at all times shall provide and furnish thee with such as will amuse and afford Instruction, as reading good authors and attending to their remarks and observations, lays a foundation to make men wise in all piety and virtue, and renders them capable of being usefull to Mankind in every Station, also gives them a knowledg of the Differant passions and propensaties of human nature in all States and conditions, therefore hope thee will endeavor to improve from reading, and lay a good foundation when thee arives to the age of Manhood Should thee be Spared. be carefull not to injure or deface the books I send thee, nor lend them on any account as the[y] often get injured going through many hands . . .[72]

By the winter of 1794, William Corbit had come to a decision to move his entire family to Philadelphia, presumably to be near schools for the boys—Edward, William Fisher, and John Cowgill—and to be in closer contact with the Philadelphia leather market.[73] Almost immediately he bought from his cousin Rachel Bettle Richards a large farm near Gray's Ferry in Passyunk Township and settled down as a tanner-farmer on the outskirts of the city.[74] The farm was on the east side of the main road leading from Philadelphia to Chester, and part of the land sloped down to the Schuylkill River. Its location was suitable for both water and land transportation to Appoquinimink, enabling Corbit to keep in touch with the business at home and at the same time to be aware of conditions in Philadelphia. He wrote his son in the summer of 1799: "by accounts from Phila^{d} the fever appears to increase which alarms the inhabitants much, many moving out . . . [we] think our Selves safe as to cetching the Disorder from our Distance from the City, as I intend have little communication from this time thare." [75]

In 1796 Pennell, having completed his training, had returned to Cantwell's Bridge to operate the tannery, and the farm in Passyunk became a headquarters from which William Corbit acted as agent for the business. He reported market conditions to his son: "I think it a good time for thee to Sell thy leather at our hous. I am told soal Leather will fetch a tolarable price. Therefore if thee has any for Sale, thee had better bring it up . . ." [76] At other times he bought hides in the city and sent them to Pennell to be tanned, together with detailed instructions: "I have Sent by Thomas Starr 103 dry hides and one hwt of lime. I expect to be at Appoquinimink by Second day next. If thee could get old Richard to assist thee in breaking in about 30 or 40 of them . . . thee might String Some on ropes in the creek on first day morning as the creek water will not answer this time of year for hides to remain tharin above thirty hours or thare abouts. Tharefore put not to soke unless they can be broke in that time. In the meantime make a new lime of about at first two bushels of lime . . ." [77]

The Corbits remained eight years in Passyunk, where William Corbit was registered as "a farmer, no slaves" in the tax list of 1800.[78] In October, 1800, they hired a three-story house at 87 South Sixth Street and spent the winter in town.[79] It was a pleasant location near the corner of Spruce Street, only two blocks from the State House; from the description made by the insurance surveyor, it would appear that the house was extremely comfortable. Paneled chimney breasts and dadoes decorated the reception rooms and bedrooms, as was the custom in Philadelphia houses of the late eighteenth century. A kitchen wing with a bedroom above extended to the rear, and windows opened onto a courtyard at the south side of the house.[80] It was apparently furnished from the unused house at Appoquinimink, for William Corbit wrote to Pennell asking that "the carpet be sent up at the first opportunity." [81]

The farm, on the other hand, had apparently been purchased as an investment; as early as 1796 Corbit had divided this land into smaller tracts, selling 9 acres that year to George Brunor, a tanner.[82] The next year he sold 17 acres along the Schuylkill River to Martin Kocker Sperger and 21 acres to Adam Zantzinger.[83] In 1798 Daniel Drinker, a Philadelphia merchant, bought a 29-acre plot adjoining the lane leading to Corbit's house.[84] The next year two innkeepers from the Northern Liberties, John Perkenpine and Jacob Baker, bought a 6-acre lot; [85] and the remaining part of the farm, including the farmhouse, was sold by the Corbits to Henry Shriver in 1807 for $20,000.[86] William Corbit had bought the entire 231-acre tract in 1795 for £3,600 and had realized £1,637 on the first five tracts sold, thus making more than a 50 per cent profit. Between the time of the sale of these lands and his death in 1817, William Corbit reinvested in Philadelphia real estate, buying the seven houses on Eighth Street in Spring Garden which he bequeathed to his daughters.[87]

When he returned to Cantwell's Bridge permanently in 1802, William Corbit was fifty-six years old, not an old man, but evidently the most respected one in town. He was rich, for he had told his son that he "could not possibly ever stand in need of money." [88] With a successful tannery, supplemented by an income from real estate in Philadelphia and farms in Delaware, this was certainly true. The manner in which he bought up farm land surrounding the bridge across the Appoquinimink suggests that William Corbit was acquiring it with the hope that the town would expand and that this waterfront property would increase in value. The land he owned on the main street of the town was divided into narrow house lots and given to his children.[89]

His possession of more than 600 acres of land enabled William Corbit to rival David Wilson, the Joneses, and the Cantwells themselves as an important landholder, while the very nature of his tanning business with its cash profits made it possible for him to help others when they needed money. In 1802 Corbit paid $1,850 against the debts of his brother-in-law, Joseph Cowgill, who had become involved in an unsuccessful partnership with architect Owen Biddle.[90] As early as 1785, John Meriss had entrusted the guardianship of his son Benjamin to "my friend William Corbit." [91] Corbit was named the executor of his brother Israel's estate; and, when his sister-in-law Ann Lea Corbit, widow of Daniel, died without completing the administration of her husband's estate, William Corbit posted £1,000 bond in security for her half brother Jonas Preston, who was appointed administrator.[92] In 1805 Corbit served as executor of the estate of his intellectual friend Cantwell Jones, the son of the justice who had officiated at his marriage to Mary Pennell some thirty years earlier.[93]

In a pattern often followed by later American businessmen, William Corbit now became interested in politics. Although Quakers were normally reluctant to take part in government (and Mary Cowgill Corbit had, in fact, expressed herself strongly when her brother voted in an election), William Corbit achieved prominence in the Federalist party.[94] Nehemiah Tilton wrote to Caesar A. Rodney concerning a speech of Thomas Jefferson's, perhaps about the purchase of Louisiana: "Wm. Corbit has declared that he is satisfied, that he has been deceived & that hereafter the man who speaks against Jefferson merits contempt; deserves and ought to be suspected of evil designs etc., etc.—as a leading Quaker & a decided fed. this augurs well." [95] Corbit remained firm in his conservatism; in 1807 he was the unsuccessful candidate of the Federal Republicans for the State Senate.[96]

William Corbit came to the end of his life respected and content. His older children were already established with families of their own in houses which he had given them; the younger children had been educated at the Friends Boarding School in Westtown, Pennsylvania.[97] His younger sons were in trade; John had been apprenticed in Birmingham, and Thomas in Philadelphia, where he could also collect the rents from the family properties.[98] His daughters, Sarah and Mary, were still at home, although Sarah was later to marry Presley Spruance of Smyrna. William Corbit spent his last days with his devoted wife, presumably supervising his business affairs, keeping in touch with his children, and reading the books he had acquired on such diverse subjects as Quaker sufferings and Bonaparte's campaigns in Egypt (see Appendix H). His son Daniel made this notation in the family Bible: "William Corbit died eight month first day 1818, aged 72 years 6 months and 11 days." It can be assumed that on this occasion John Janvier, the town cabinetmaker and undertaker, brought out his two-wheeled hearse, always reserved for the more important funerals. Thus, in the summer heat, William Corbit made his last trip through the town which had been his home for more than fifty years and was laid to rest in the burying ground beside the Friends Meeting House at the western end of Main Street.

Notes to Chapter 2

1. "Records of Duck Creek Monthly Meeting, 1687-1896," *Collections of the Genealogical Society of Pennsylvania*, CCXLI (1909), entry made May 9, 1717.

2. New Castle County Deeds, Book H, Fol. 131, and Book G, Fol. 529; J. Thomas Scharf, *History of Delaware*, p. 1015. The farm was sold in 1800 by Daniel Corbit's great-grandson, Joseph Corbit, a Philadelphia house carpenter, and later passed into the hands of Samuel Thomas. It was repurchased by John Cowgill Corbit in the 1880's; was inherited by his sons, Alexander and Daniel Corbit; and was purchased from the estate of Daniel Corbit in 1940 by his niece, Ann Corbit Reese, in whose possession it remains.

3. Historical Society of Delaware, Corbit-Higgins-Spruance Papers, Fol. 1, MS copy of original will written December 12, 1755.

4. Public Archives Commission of the State of Delaware, New Castle County Inventories 1758. Hereafter cited as Delaware Archives.

5. Corbit-Higgins-Spruance Papers, Will of Daniel Corbit.

6. Janetta Wright Schoonover, *A History of William Brinton* (Trenton, New Jersey, 1924), p. 153.

7. Duck Creek MM, I, 82 (March 17, 1729).

8. Delaware Archives, Administration Papers of Caleb Offley, July 28, 1729.

9. Caleb Offley had married Eliza England in 1722 (Duck Creek MM, I, 41); New Castle County Wills, Book Misc., I, 373.

10. Duck Creek MM, I, 106 (August 22, 1737); "Records of Duck Creek MM," p. 87 (August 30, 1743).

11. Corbit-Higgins-Spruance Papers, Will of Daniel Corbit.

12. Marriage Certificate of Daniel and Mary Corbit, November 8, 1739, MS in the possession of Mrs. Charles Lee Reese, Jr.

13. Mary Corbit Warner, *Brinton-Corbit Book* (Wilmington, 1907), p. 16; Schoonover, *op. cit.*, p. 101.

14. Duck Creek MM, I, 171 (December 18, 1752).

15. Corbit-Higgins-Spruance Papers, Will of Daniel Corbit.

16. Schoonover, *op. cit.*, p. 127.

17. *Ibid.*, p. 131.

18. Chester County Historical Society, MS 1926.

19. Duck Creek MM, I, 226 (July 26, 1760).

20. New Castle County Wills, Book K, I, 128.

21. Israel and Mary Humphries Corbit acknowledged their "outgoings in marriage" before Duck Creek Monthly Meeting, September 28, 1771; William Corbit acknowledged his "marriage with the assistance of a magistrate" before the Meeting on November 24, 1781; Mary Corbit Wilson was testified against by the Women Friends of Duck Creek on August 26, 1769, for marrying a "man not of our Society and with the assistance of a priest" (Duck Creek MM). Daniel Corbit and Ann Lea were married out of meeting in 1775. See James Henry Lea, *The Ancestry and Posterity of John Lea* (Philadelphia, 1906), p. 15.

22. Duck Creek MM, I, 285 (May 26, 1765).

23. Genealogical Society of Pennsylvania, "Minutes of Philadelphia Monthly Meetings 1730-1785," entries made August 30, 1765, and March 27, 1767.

24. *Staatsbote* (Philadelphia), No. 632, March 1, 1774.

25. *Pennsylvania Chronicle*, No. 327, April 19, 1773.

26. *Staatsbote, loc. cit.*

27. Malachy Postlethwayt, *The Universal Dictionary of Trade and Commerce* [London, 1755], II, 36; *The Charter, Laws, and Catalogue of Books, of the Library Company of Philadelphia* [Philadelphia, 1770].

28. J. Leander Bishop, *A History of American Manufactures 1608-1860* (Philadelphia, 1864), I, 461.

29. Corbit Papers (in the custody of the heirs of Sara Corbit Levis), Deed, David Wilson *et uxor* to William Corbit, February 16, 1771.

30. Edgar T. Wherry, "Notes on the Vegetation of Delaware," *Delaware, a History of the First State*, I, 18; *Pennsylvania Gazette*, No. 2364, April 13, 1774.

31. David Wilson Mansion, Inc., "Ledger, 1766-1771," Fol. 271.

32. Bishop, *op. cit.*, I, 453.

33. Temple Henry Croker, Thomas Williams, and Samuel Clark, *The Complete Dictionary of Arts and Sciences* [London, 1766], "Tanning."

34. Corbit-Higgins-Spruance Papers, Fol. 4, William Corbit to Pennell Corbit, Appoquinimink, September 21, 1796.

35. *Ibid.*, William Corbit to Pennell Corbit, Appoquinimink, March 9, 1801.

36. *Ibid.*, Fol. I, Land Survey, Philip Reading, September 3, 1783.

37. *Documents Relative to the Manufactures in the United States* (*Executive Documents*, 22nd Congress, 1st Session, No. 308) (Washington, 1833), II, 756.

38. Duck Creek MM, I, 308 (November 28, 1767). The testimony was published January 23, 1768.

39. Corbit Papers, MS genealogical data copied for Mary Corbit Warner from the Wilson family Bible, Richmond, Indiana, and from the records of Friends Meeting House, Sixteenth and Race Streets, Philadelphia, n.d.

40. Duck Creek MM, I, 352, 361 (August 24, 1771, to March 28, 1772).

41. New Castle County Wills, Book K, I, 128.

42. Corbit Papers, Marriage Certificate of William Corbit and Mary Pennell, February 19, 1773.

43. Carl and Jessica Bridenbaugh, *Rebels and Gentlemen; Philadelphia in the Age of Franklin* (New York, 1942), p. 181. Jack MacPherson made this remark at the time of Polly Norris' marriage to John Dickinson, referring pointedly to the bride's personal fortune of £50,000.

44. Corbit-Higgins-Spruance Papers, Fol. 1, Trustee's Account of Mary Pennell's inheritance, 1752-1773; Scharf, *op. cit.*, p. 991.

45. Gilbert Cope, *Genealogy of Smedley Family* (Lancaster, Pennsylvania, 1901), p. 191.

46. Chester County Deeds, Book V, p. 419; Book T, p. 526; Chester County Wills, Box 1306.

47. Delaware Archives, Marriage Records, LXXXVII, 171; Duck Creek MM, I, 349 (June 22, 1771).

48. New Castle County Wills, Book K, I, 4.

49. Corbit Papers, Marriage Certificate of William Corbit and Mary Pennell.

50. Corbit family Bible, in the possession of Mrs. D. Meredith Reese.

51. Corbit-Higgins-Spruance Papers, Fol. 1, Corbit Genealogy.

52. Schoonover, *op. cit.*, p. 156.

53. Corbit family papers in the possession of Mrs. D. Meredith Reese (hereafter cited as Ann Corbit Reese Papers), Deed, James Moor and wife to William Corbit, June 15, 1775.

54. Ann Corbit Reese Papers, Receipts to William Corbit (March 1, 1777, to August 22, 1777).

55. *Ibid.*, Deed, Jonathan Wilson and wife to William Corbit, March 2, 1783.

56. Scharf, *op. cit.*, p. 1007.

57. Delaware Archives, Fol. 160, Oaths of Allegiance.

58. Duck Creek MM, I, 401 (May 27, 1775).

59. *Ibid.*, II, 1-3 (November 24, 1781; December 22, 1781).

60. *Ibid.*, II, 50 (June 26, 1784).

61. *Ibid.*, II, 58 (November 27, 1784); Corbit Bible.

62. John A. H. Sweeney, "The Norris-Fisher Correspondence: A Circle of Friends, 1779-82," *Delaware History*, VI (March, 1955).

63. Corbit-Higgins-Spruance Papers, Fol. 3, M. Dickinson to Sarah Corbit, n.d.

64. Corbit Bible.

65. Corbit-Higgins-Spruance Papers, Will of William Corbit, August 11, 1817.

66. Corbit Papers, Marriage Certificate of William Corbit and Mary Cowgill, April 28, 1791.

67. Corbit Bible.

68. Duck Creek MM, II, 163 (May 2, 1792).

69. Corbit-Higgins-Spruance Papers, Fol. 4, William Corbit to Pennell Corbit, Philadelphia, n.d.

70. *Ibid.*, William Corbit to Pennell Corbit, Philadelphia, n.d.

71. *Ibid.*, William Corbit to Pennell Corbit, Philadelphia, May 8, 1790.

72. *Ibid.*, William Corbit to Pennell Corbit, Philadelphia, n.d.

73. Duck Creek MM, II, 190 (November, 1794).

74. Corbit-Higgins-Spruance Papers, Deed, Rachel Richards *et al.* to William Corbit, February 12, 1795. The land is in the vicinity of Thirty-Fifth and Wharton Streets, near Gray's Ferry Avenue, and is now an industrial site.

75. *Ibid.*, William Corbit to Pennell Corbit, Appoquinimink, August 8, 1799.

76. *Ibid.*, William Corbit to Pennell Corbit, Appoquinimink, October 29, 1799.

77. *Ibid.*, William Corbit to Pennell Corbit, Appoquinimink, August 31, 1796.

78. Historical Society of Pennsylvania, MSS, "List of the Taxable Inhabitants residing within the County of Philadelphia . . . 1800," p. 180.

79. Corbit-Higgins-Spruance Papers, Fol. 4, William Corbit to Pennell Corbit, October 24, 1800; Letter from Dr. Robert W. Shoemaker, U. S. National Park Service, August 17, 1953.

80. Mutual Assurance Company (Philadelphia), Survey and Policy No. 539, September, 1792.

81. Corbit-Higgins-Spruance Papers, Fol. 4, William Corbit to Pennell Corbit, Appoquinimink, December 6, 1800.

82. Philadelphia County Deeds, Book D, No. 57, p. 188.

83. *Ibid.*, Book D, No. 61, p. 336; Book EF, No. 6, p. 493.

84. *Ibid.*, Book EF, No. 15, p. 203.

85. *Ibid.*, Book EF, No. 7, p. 264.

86. *Ibid.*, Book EF, No. 24, p. 587.

87. Corbit-Higgins-Spruance Papers, Will of William Corbit.

88. *Ibid.*, Fol. 5, autobiographical notes in the handwriting of William Fisher Corbit, n.d.

89. *Ibid.*, Will of William Corbit.

90. *Ibid.*, Fol. 4, William Corbit to Miers Fisher, Philadelphia, July 8, 1802. Joseph Cowgill sold Corbit his house in Powell Street for $1650 on March 2, 1802 (Philadelphia Deeds, Book IC, No. 9, p. 42). Corbit sold the house to John Douglass, a cabinetmaker, on October 1, 1802, for $1750 (Corbit Papers, Deed, William Corbit and wife to John Douglass). The house apparently reverted to Corbit, for he sold it again to Edward Wilson, merchant, on April 20, 1804 (Philadelphia Deeds, Book IC, No. 9, pp. 43-44). Corbit probably took the house as collateral for the money he advanced Cowgill; he never lived in the house, and in 1802 it was occupied by Mrs. Anna M'Culloh (*Philadelphia Directory, 1802*).

91. Corbit-Higgins-Spruance Papers, Fol. 14, copy of Will of John Meriss, 1785.

92. New Castle County Wills, Book N, I, 21, 28.

93. Papers of Mrs. Paul J. Nowland (Louise Corbit Lea), Inventory of Cantwell Jones, August 20, 1805. This large estate, appraised at $10,284.53, included a library of more than 140 volumes.

94. Corbit-Higgins-Spruance Papers, Mary Cowgill to John Cowgill, November 10, 1788.

95. Historical Society of Delaware, Rodney Collection, Nehemiah Tilton to C. A. Rodney, Washington, October 27, 1803.

96. *Museum of Delaware* (Wilmington), September 26, 1807.

97. Records of Westtown Friends School, letter from Susanna Smedley, Historical Librarian, Westtown, Pennsylvania, April 17, 1954.

98. Corbit-Higgins-Spruance Papers, Fol. 5, John C. Corbit to William Corbit, Appoquinimink, May 18, 1807; Fol. 6, Thomas Corbit to Daniel Corbit, Appoquinimink, September 17, 1819.

N 41 E. 9 Pr. 19 Lk.

N 4½ W. 4 Pr. 21 Lk.

Lot of Ground

Pr 46 Perches

S 4½ E. 4 Pr. 21 Lk.

The Above described Lot of Ground situate & lying in St Georges Hundred & County of New Castle on Delaware near Apoquimimink Bridge & on the N. W. side of sd Road to the Landing & Tan Yard Beginning in the sd Road & near the Eastmost Corner of Mr William Corbit's Dwelling House thence with sd Road S 41° W. 9 perches 14 Links to a Corner stone thence N 4½ W. 4 Pr. 21 Links to a Co. stone thence N 41 E. 9 Prs 19 Lks thence with the North Eastmost end of sd House S 4½ E. 4 Pr. 21 Lks to the Beginning Containing Forty six Perches of Land

Surveyed for Mr William Corbit the 9th Day of June 1777

pr Philip Reading

Survey of the Corbit Property, 1777, from the original document in the Ann Corbit Reese Papers

Chapter 3

The House

The house William Corbit began to build in 1772 at the age of twenty-seven was his home for more than forty years and is the real record of his life. In it is seen that same combination of practical tradesman and cultured gentleman which seems to mark William Corbit's personality. The tanner's house was an important unit in the eighteenth-century tannery, and advertisements for the sale of tanyards often included a large house. A tanyard offered for sale in Philadelphia in 1786 was described as Corbit's might have been: ". . . there are also on the premises, a good brick dwelling house, with two rooms on the first floor, and four on the second, with a brick kitchen, and a handsome garden walled in with brick and capped with stone; likewise, a stable sufficient for 3 or 4 horses, a fodder and chair house; the whole of the buildings are covered with cedar shingles, and are in very good order." [1]

It was not unusual in the eighteenth century for a fine house to be as close as was the Corbit House to a factory-type operation that was at best unpleasant, if not also unsightly. With his home only a few hundred yards from his tanyard, Corbit could be close to his business at all times. It is to his credit that, in building a house that served such a practical function in connection with his means of making a living, William Corbit built the handsomest one for miles around. His experience in Philadelphia had made him aware of quality in architecture, and he simulated the elegance of a town house in his mansion in a country town.

Early in 1777 Corbit bought from his brother-in-law, David Wilson, the land upon which the house stood; and on June 9 had Philip Reading,

The Corbit House, parlor

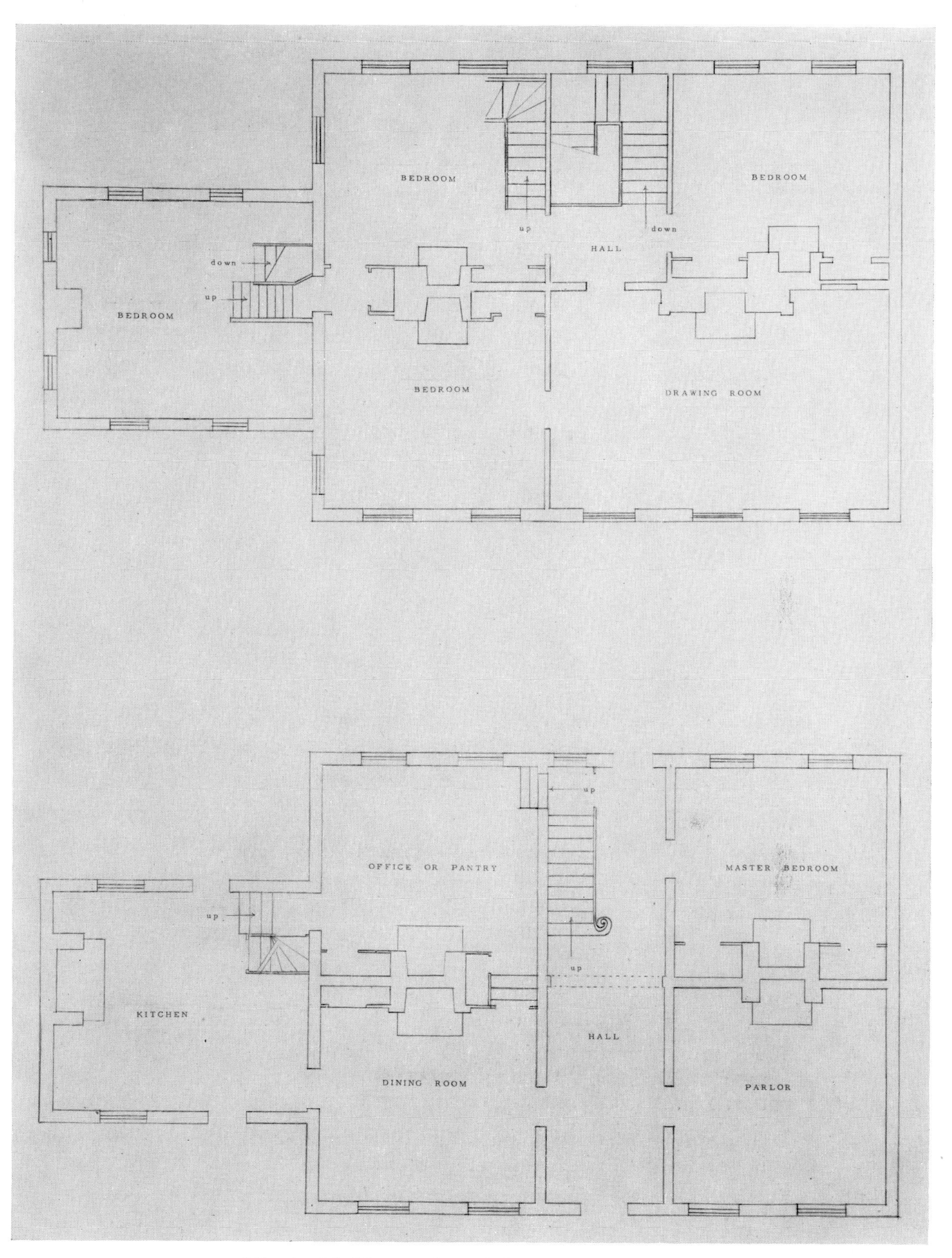

The Corbit House, plan of first and second floors

son of the rector of St. Anne's Church at nearby Middletown, draw up a survey of the lot.[2] Reading included in one corner of the survey a sketch of the house, which shows it as it was at that time. A square building with a low hip roof topped by a balustraded "roof-deck" and ridge chimneys, the house stood at the edge of the lot facing the road which led to the landing and tanyard. Built of brick laid in Flemish bond, the house possesses distinguished structural refinements in a molded water table, granite belt course, and carved granite window lintels. The pedimented doorway, into which an arched transom is cut, is a fine example of the Doric type described by Thomas Waterman as the "Philadelphia-style," and is almost identical with the doorway of the famed Stamper-Blackwell House on Pine Street in Philadelphia.[3]

Following a Delaware custom, white paneled shutters frame the windows of the lower story, while green louvered blinds, similar to those on the entrance door, are used for the second-story windows. A handsome cornice with carved mutule blocks and decorated soffit crowns the façade; foliated wooden consoles frame the arched dormer windows; and an intricate latticework railing surrounds the roof-deck. At a later date, a two-story wing, containing a kitchen and additional bedroom space, was added to the south side of the house; louvered doors at front and back give access to this wing.[4] The house was originally perched on a narrow terrace from which five granite steps descended to the road leading to the tanyard.

The house has a center hall and four rooms on the ground floor. Importance is given to the hallway by the use of pedimented doorframes and a paneled dado that complement a cornice of a modified Roman Doric order. Midway in the depth of the hall, a lintel, finished as a full Doric entablature, is supported by fluted pilasters, forming an arch which frames the stairway to the second floor. On one side of the hall is the parlor, a simple and dignified room, originally painted a soft moss green which has now been duplicated on the woodwork and plaster walls. The chimney breast projects from the paneled fireplace wall, and an overmantel frame with crossetted corners provides a background for a picture, repeating at the same time the crossetted corners of the molding around the fireplace opening. A dentil molding decorates the mantel shelf and is repeated in the cornice encircling the room. Two windows on the front wall of the room looked on to the road to the tanyard. Behind the parlor, with windows facing the side of David Wilson's house, is a simply paneled room used as a bedroom, according to the inventory of the house made in 1818—presumably the master bedroom.[5]

Across the hall from the parlor is the dining room, with paneling almost matching that of the parlor. Here, beside the fireplace, is a china cupboard and beneath it a sliding candle tray, for which the carpenter charged William Corbit seven shillings sixpence.[6] Between the two front windows a Duncan Beard clock now stands where William Corbit probably kept the "Clock & Case in the Dineing Room" mentioned in his inventory.[7] Up a short flight of steps from the dining room is a room perhaps used as a pantry or office. The woodwork here was not painted and the walls were whitewashed; a ventilator in the floor permitted heat to come up from the original kitchen in the cellar beneath. Access to the kitchen was gained by stairs opening off this room and descending under the main stairway of the house. The later kitchen is on the ground level and opens directly into the dining room.

On the second floor are three bedrooms, all finished with fielded paneling on the fireplace wall, two with plain ovolo moldings around the fireplace openings and one with a mantel. Across the front of the house is a great room, formed by including the width of the hallway in the space allotted for the northeast room. This large room, the most elaborate in the house and in striking contrast to the bedrooms, was patterned after the ballroom of a Philadelphia or southern mansion and was perhaps intended to be used as a drawing room, although at the time of William Corbit's death it was being used as a bedroom and was referred to by his children as "the long room." [8] The chimney breast is framed by fluted pilasters, which support an entablature and modillioned cornice extending around the room. The overmantel frame is surmounted by a broken pediment, repeated by the pediments of the balancing doors which flank the fireplace. A fret-carved base molding and chair rail add distinction to the wainscoting of the room, and applied moldings outline the sunk plaster fields on the side walls. Three recessed windows opposite the fireplace wall flood the room with daylight. From one of the rear bedrooms a narrow staircase twists up to the third floor, where three small bedrooms under the sloping eaves open onto a square hall. Out of this hall a ladder leads to the roof-deck, from which William Corbit could survey the activity at the tanyard and the landing, and could look across the Appoquinimink to his meadows and wheat fields.

The practical strain dominant in William Corbit's character that had enabled him to amass so much property is reflected in the record he kept of the expenses incurred in building his house.[9] This account, now in the collections of the Historical Society of Delaware, not only itemizes minutely the exact cost of the house but also reveals the story of its construction. The scope of the project is indicated by the first entry: £89 2*s.* 3*d.* for 89,250 bricks at 20 shillings per thousand. These bricks were perhaps made by the local brickmaker who had made the bricks that David Wilson used when he built his own house two years before.[10] Much of the other material used in the house was brought in by ship, unloaded at the landing, and hauled up the hill to the building site. This fact in itself is an important comment upon the economy of Appoquinimink as well as a reflection of the tastes and contacts of William Corbit.

An entry of £3 against "Stone from Chester" indicates that some of the stone used in the cellar or in the window lintels was brought down the river from Chester. The cost of hauling the stone for the cellar was more than £7, while the cost of laying it came to £20 8*s.* 9*d.*; thus transportation charges figure as a large part of the expense of the house. The names of shipmasters—John Bryans and Isaac and Thomas Starr—occur again and again as agents carrying boatloads of lumber, casks of nails, and boxes of window glass. Pine and cedar boards were bought in enormous quantities, with one consignment of 1,000 feet from Wetherill & Cresson, a Philadelphia lumber firm.[11]

Other materials were purchased from David and Abraham Van Dyke, William Walker, Samuel Young, Samuel Floyd, and Nicholas Sellers, some of whom were among the builders of Old Drawyers Church.[12] In fact, some of the lumber was purchased at this meeting house, which was being rebuilt at the same time. A few later entries reveal the sources of some of the accessories: hinges and screws from Wilmington; locks and hinges from James Bringhurst, a prominent Philadelphia hardware merchant; and nails and locks from Dickson & Millins. The final entry in Corbit's account of "expences" noted payment to David Wilson for "Iron back & Jaums," £5 7*s.* 4*d.*; the total cost was set down as £1,374 11*s.* 9*d.*

A corps of workmen must have been needed to carry on the building of this great house, but William Corbit's account mentions few by name. Joseph Stride did the painting and, according to one entry, charged £13 9*s.* for "Oyl & Whitelead & paints." The total cost of painting for the house, including materials, Stride's labor, and his board, amounted to more than £45 and indicates that painted walls would have been a luxury in many colonial homes. An entry for "120 Qts. of White lead . . . 8 gallons oyll 3/4 hundred whiting & other paints" suggests that the trim of the house was originally painted white. The only other workman listed is Richard Lippincot, who built an oven and turned some of the trimmers in the floor framing. The joiners, with whom William Corbit contracted to supply all the woodwork, are known only through the man who presented their bill.

The dates in the margin of the building account provide a chronological history of the construction of the house. Begun in the spring or early summer of 1772, the house was slow in rising. The bricks were laid by July, but the roof was not shingled until the following April. When Mary Pennell became Mrs. Corbit, her house was only a shell, although the glass for the windows was soon ordered. By May, 1773, the roof-deck had been covered with lead; within a month the shingles were oiled, the windows glazed, and part of the painting completed. By Christmas the plastering was partially finished. In 1774 the front steps were built, the brick wall in front of the house was laid, more windows hung, more woodwork painted, the plastering completed, and the locks and hinges fitted on the doors. In August of that year the joiners finished their work; and late in the fall, as soon as Joseph Stride had finished the painting, the house was ready for the Corbits.

Although Robert May and Company presented their bill August 10,

1774, their workmen had been engaged at the Corbit House for more than a year.[13] They had begun their work with the shingling of the roof and finished it by making the shutters. The bill, totaling £563 14*s*., records in detail the basic and ornamental woodwork, with its size and its cost. While William Corbit's account of expenses presents a narrative of the building of the house and suggests the sources of the materials, Robert May's bill, by its language, provides the contemporary names of architectural details and indirectly shows the working habits of master craftsmen in the late eighteenth century. The bill appears to be outlined chronologically, although only the final date is given; and the billing for the woodwork is listed according to each room from the top down. Thus, from the bill a picture can be drawn of the carpenters' work as they proceeded day by day from room to room.

Once they had framed-in the roof and shingled it, the carpenters made a flooring for the roof-deck, or "terrass," and surrounded it with a railing of "Chineas Lattis." They worked in advance of the plasterers, putting up the rough partitions and covering them with laths for plastering, later returning to make the baseboards, doorframes, and other trim. Then the joiners carefully constructed the paneling for which the Corbit House is famous. Fielded panels covered the fireplace wall of each room, and cornices, "bases and surbases" trimmed the other walls—bases being the capping molding of the skirting or baseboards, and surbases the chair rails. In the parlor and entrance hall, wainscoting reached from the base to the chair rail.

Robert May wrote up the bill himself in the careful handwriting that is identical to that found in his only known signatures. While the terminology of the bill provides a clue to the contemporary description of architectural features, it also reflects the academic training of Robert May. On the whole, the items were correctly listed, corresponding to the definitions given in such general handbooks as *The Builder's Dictionary*.[14] One of the most frequent terms used is "arch^{v}," an abbreviation for architrave, and used in reference to the lowest part of a horizontal molding, whether in a cornice, door trim, window frame, or chimney opening. May goes on to list "dentle cornice" in the parlor and dining room at the cost of 2 shillings one penny per foot; fluted pilasters at 2 shillings sixpence per foot and a "Cornice with Mutules" in the hallway; and a "modillion cornice" at 2 shillings sixpence in the second-floor drawing room.

The square panels formed of ovolo moldings with crossetted corners (described as "knees") used in the overmantel frames in the parlor, dining room, and drawing room were described by May as "tabernacle frames." This term is not entirely correct, for the English architect Robert Adam, writing a year earlier (1773), considered the tabernacle frame to consist of a pediment supported by applied columns, the whole feature placed against a wall and giving the impression of a large religious tabernacle.[15] May was perhaps using a generally accepted vernacular meaning, for Gunning Bedford, in writing the insurance survey of the Powel House in Philadelphia, described the overmantel treatments, which are similar to those in the Corbit House, as "Chimney Brest tabernakle." [16] The overmantel in the Corbit drawing room was surmounted by a feature lifted from a conventional tabernacle frame, a broken pediment which matches those over the doorways, supplied at a price of £3 apiece. This decoration again reflects a vernacular taste, for architectural writers of the eighteenth century decried the broken pediment as an impossible feature borrowed from a structural context and used without meaning in a decorative context. The front doorway of the Corbit House, combining such classical details as Tuscan columns supporting a Doric entablature and pediment with the architectural whimsy of a "Gothick" sash in the transom window, was listed impressively as a "frontispiece" and cost a total of £18.

The carpenter's bill includes every item of woodwork in the house—the floor boards, the stairs, the newel boards, the mantels, doors, windows, and even the bars for the cellar windows and the "pallisade fence" for the back yard. In the building of country houses in England, local labor usually performed the general work, and joiners were often imported from London to put in the paneling; such was the case at the Corbit House.[17] The carpenters came to Cantwell's Bridge probably a year after the house was begun, installed all the woodwork, presented their bill, and left. Nothing has been heard of them since, and the invoice presented to William Corbit is the only known record of Robert May and Company.

Traditions have grown up and suppositions have been put forth as to the mysterious figure who apparently designed the Corbit House and placed in it some of the most beautiful woodwork in colonial American architecture. Tradition speaks of "Robert May and Company of London" as a type of architectural mail-order house, which sent William Corbit the plans for his house and possibly supplied the workmen to carry them out. It is now known that Robert May was an individual who was in the vicinity of Cantwell's Bridge when the house was being built. When William Corbit and Mary Pennell were married in 1773, Robert May was among the guests at the wedding and signed the marriage certificate.[18] A year later, on March 25, 1774, William Corbit's father hurriedly drew up his will, neglecting to mention his son, and signed the paper in the presence of Jonathan Wilson, Joseph Hanson, both of Appoquinimink Hundred, and Robert May.[19] These documents record May as having been in America, but anything further said about him is conjecture. His name is not included among the 500 or more accounts in David Wilson's ledger, although a number of Wilson's customers were identified as carpenters. No Robert May appears in the tax lists of New Castle County, but a Frances May was counted among the taxables of Appoquinimink Hundred from 1778 until 1783.[20] Whether she was his widow is not known.

The public records of the Philadelphia area contain no mention of an architect or house carpenter by the name of Robert May, and he was not listed as a member of the Carpenters' Company.[21] However, information from other sources forms the basis for a theory about his identity. In 1792 Thomas May, a Wilmington merchant, died, leaving £300 to his brother Robert and appointing him executor of his estate.[22] As early as 1762, Thomas May had been an ironmaster and proprietor of the iron furnaces at Elk Forge in Cecil County, Maryland.[23] He mentioned in his ledger that he had to induce his brother Robert to act as superintendent of the company's business at Elk Forge from 1781 until 1790 by paying him "much more" than the standard salary of £100 a year.[24] What other occupation may have attracted Robert May is not disclosed. It is known, however, that he was living at Head of Elk during this period, for he was listed as a resident of that village when he subscribed to the publication of John Varlo's *A New System of Husbandry* in 1785.

After the death of his brother, Robert May and his cousin, John Brooke, administered the estate; in the *Philadelphia Gazette* of December 26, 1799, they advertised the sale of part of Elk Forge, 1,750 acres of land, a 132-acre farm on the Elk River, and a lot, wharf, and warehouse in Elkton. Two years later, however, Robert May, described as a yeoman from Chester County, Pennsylvania, formed a partnership with John and Stephen Hayes and Joshua Seal, Wilmington merchants, and, as the firm of Robert May and Company, operated Elk Forge.[25] It is possible, but by no means certain, that this Robert May, who was born in Philadelphia County in 1750, the son of Robert May and Elizabeth Brooke, had been a merchant who had contracted to supply building materials to William Corbit, and had later gone into business with his brother, a merchant-ironmaster.[26]

Whoever Robert May was—if, indeed, he was the architect of the Corbit House—he unquestionably had contact with Philadelphia, and his experience illustrates once again the close relationship of Cantwell's Bridge to that city. The Corbit House is a city house in form and in decoration. While its square mass, hip roof, and roof-deck are related to such country houses near Philadelphia as Mount Pleasant and Woodford, its fenestration and the concentration of ornament on the façade resemble that of such town houses as the Samuel Powel House, 244 South Third Street, Philadelphia, or the Deschler House in Germantown; in both houses the interior woodwork is remarkably like that of the Corbit House. William Corbit must have been well acquainted with the Philadelphia town house after spending two years in the city. It may not be mere coincidence that the Corbit House originally sat on a terrace facing a street and, like a row house, had a solid north wall and only two windows in the south wall. It is possible that William Corbit conceived of Cantwell's Bridge as a future city; if so, the style of his house would have been entirely appropriate. If Cantwell's Bridge had become another great port like Philadelphia, the Corbit House would have occupied a prominent and valuable position on the first street above the harbor.

The similarity of the Corbit House to the Powel House in Philadelphia is extraordinary and has been the cause of much speculation. Not only does the Corbit House resemble the Powel House (built about 1765 by Charles Stedman) in the decoration of its façade, but details of the interior woodwork are identical, and the second-floor drawing room is so similar to the great drawing room of the Philadelphia house that it served as a model for the restoration of the Powel drawing room when the latter was removed to the Philadelphia Museum of Art.[27] The plan of the Corbit room, featuring a projecting chimney breast framed by fluted pilasters and flanked by pedimented doorways, is identical to that of the Powel room, which, however, was altered slightly when it was installed in the Museum. The Corbit room is smaller and lacks some of the embellishments of the Powel room—the rococo frieze, decorated plaster ceiling, armorial cartouche in the overmantel pediment, and mahogany doors—and possibly suggests Quaker solidity in contrast to the elegance of the room designed for Ann Graeme Stedman.[28]

In concept, if not in detail, the Corbit drawing room is also similar to the parlor of the Stamper-Blackwell House at 224 Pine Street, Philadelphia (built in 1764), now installed at The Henry Francis du Pont Winterthur Museum.[29] Here again, pedimented doors flank a projecting chimney breast richly carved with rococo decoration inspired by the same design source as the Corbit House. In addition to this similarity, the doorways of the two houses are identical. The point of communication among these three houses has not yet been determined. Possibly William Corbit knew of the Philadelphia houses, for both were important new buildings when he was apprenticed in the city. However, it is unlikely that Corbit would have had social connections with the Powels, the Stedmans, or Mayor John Stamper, for they were of the aristocratic Anglican set in Philadelphia, and he was at that time a rather plain Quaker. On the other hand, Robert May could have seen either of these important houses, perhaps through a professional association as a carpenter-architect, or, assum-

The Corbit House Drawing Room

The Powel House Drawing Room, as installed in the
Philadelphia Museum of Art

ing him to have been Robert May of Head of Elk, he or his brother might have known Charles Stedman, who was also an ironmaster.[30] Robert May perhaps had social connections in Philadelphia, for in 1786 he married Rebecca Potts, the niece of Joseph Potts, who had married Samuel Powel's sister in 1768.[31]

All of these assumptions are without verification; the only certain tie between the Delaware and Philadelphia houses is in the common source of the designs used. Fiske Kimball has treated this subject in his article, "The Sources of 'Philadelphia Chippendale,' " in which he points out that Abraham Swan's *The British Architect* (London, 1745), and his later volumes, *Designs in Architecture* (London, 1757), were available in Philadelphia at the time these houses were being built.[32] Not only were the books in the collection of the Library Company and available to the members of the Carpenters' Company in their own library, but they had been available to the general public at James Rivington's bookstore as early as 1760.[33] William Corbit could have seen these books himself while he was in Philadelphia, for his master was a member of the Library Company. It can be assumed with certainty, however, that the designer, or master builder, of the Corbit House had one of Swan's books in his traveling bag when he came down to Cantwell's Bridge to supervise the construction of Mr. Corbit's mansion.

Fiske Kimball notes that Swan's book was the first important English book to show the French mode in architecture.[34] It is almost a paradox that the designer of the Corbit House scraped off the French, or *rocaille*, ornament in Swan's designs and executed a simplified version of the basically Palladian forms underneath. Thus, the mantel and overmantel in the Corbit parlor are derived from Plate L in Swan's *British Architect*, and other features in the house are similarly adapted.[35]

In the preface of his second book, *Designs in Architecture*, Swan stated that he supposed "some less expensive designs may be acceptable to the Public," and on Plate 1 he presented the elevation and plan of a house which might well be the prototype of the Corbit House.[36] The design of the house shows four rooms on a floor, a five-bay façade with a belt course, a hip roof, and a Tuscan-order temple-doorway. A projecting

Detail of
cornice molding,
Powel House
Drawing Room

Detail of
chair-rail molding,
Corbit House
Drawing Room

Detail of
base molding,
Corbit House
Drawing Room

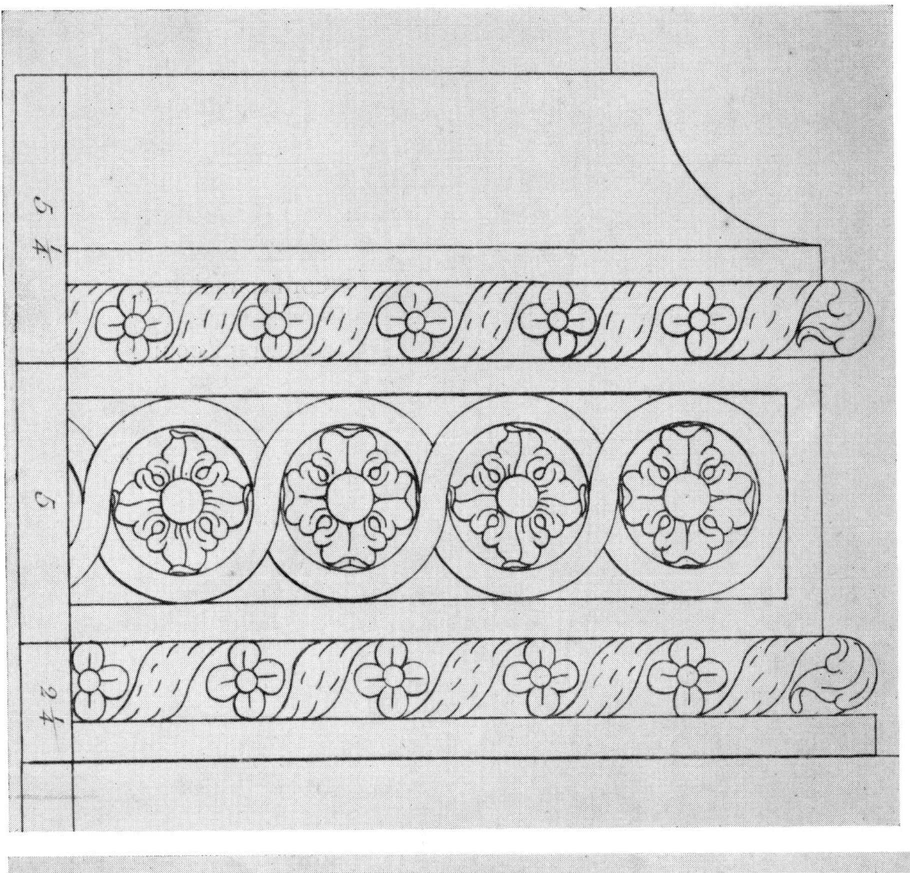

Detail, Plate 32, Swan's *Designs in Architecture.* Possible source of design for base molding, Corbit House Drawing Room

Detail, Plate 40, Swan's *Designs in Architecture.* Possible source of design for chair-rail molding, Corbit House Drawing Room

Plate 23, Swan's *Designs in Architecture*. Possible source for design of Corbit House Drawing Room

central portico is the only element not repeated in the Corbit House. The plan shown by Swan (with the exception of a secondary stairway) suggests the disposition of the rooms on the second floor of the Corbit House, and a succeeding plate (Plate 11), also a design for a house with four rooms on a floor, might be considered the prototype for the plan of the first floor of the Corbit House. In more detail, the carving in the entablature of the entrance hall of the Corbit House was inspired by Plate IV of Swan's *British Architect*, which illustrates "the Doric order." The carved decoration on the soffit of the cornice across the front of the house is also adapted from this plate.[37]

The treatment of the three windows in the second-floor drawing room, the arrangement of the panels in that room, and the broken pediment over a crossetted overmantel frame are found in Plate 23 of the *Designs*.[38] Details of the fret carving in the drawing room were gathered from various plates: the double Greek key in the capitals of the pilasters comes from Plate 26; the guilloche in the baseboard from Plate 32; and the chair-rail fret, substituting a lozenge design for foliage, derives from Plate 40.[39] These last two details were also employed in the Powel House drawing room and are identical in size. The lozenge-shaped decoration in the chair rail of the Corbit House is used in a carved band on the soffit of the cornice in the Philadelphia room; a more accurate rendering of this unusual detail is in the pulpit of Christ Church in Philadelphia, carved in 1770 by John Folwell.[40]

As with most American craftsmen, the carpenters of the Corbit House modified the imaginative creations of Swan to suit the scale and temper of the house they were building, and in doing so followed the instructions of Swan himself: "If neither this, nor any of the following, Designs, should exactly suit the Size of your Rooms, the Dimensions may be easily enlarged or contracted so as to suit your size." [41] American builders combined old forms with new styles, as shown in the projecting chimney breast of the drawing room and parlor, which was a holdover from an earlier period. Robert May's carpenters selected decorations as they pleased, using Chinese, Gothic, and classical ornament on a building basically Palladian in form. They simplified even their Philadelphia model, for this was a country house and its owner was a Quaker, who conceivably subscribed to the often mentioned aesthetic principle "of the best sort but plain."

The distinctive character which these carpenters gave to the Corbit House is reflected in a number of simpler buildings in the vicinity. In the David Wilson House (*c.* 1769), the Moore House across Appoquinimink Creek (*c.* 1773), and Old Drawyers Church (1773-1776) can be seen the same use of brick and contrasting white woodwork treated in the sculptural fullness of a "country baroque." These three buildings have traditionally been attributed to the firm of Robert May. The attribution may be well grounded on the basis of style, but no documentary proof exists.

The Wilson House had been built two or three years before the Corbit House by William Corbit's brother-in-law, David Wilson. On December 25, 1770, Wilson credited Samuel Lafever with £16 7*s.* 3*d.* for "Making & burning 77^{m} Bricks at 4/3 per 1/2 thousand," and it is possible that this was a payment for the bricks used in his house.[42] Other entries to Samuel Floyd, Miles Cain, a painter, and James Wilson, a joiner, indicate that David Wilson was doing a considerable amount of building in 1769 and 1770.[43] Since Corbit and Wilson were often in close contact, it is not unlikely that William Corbit hired the same master builder to construct his own house. (The Wilson House is now open to the public as the David Wilson Mansion and also includes the reading rooms of the Corbit Library, the first free library in Delaware.)

The other two buildings are not so closely related. No construction records exist for the Moore House, now owned by Mr. and Mrs. George F. Kelly, but an approximate date of 1773 has been made from a study of the deeds to the property.[44] In form and in plan this house is related to the Wilson House. The five-bay façade with its modillioned cornice and white window trim is similar, although the entrance door is less elaborate and is covered by a porch, which is probably a later addition. Inside, one large room is placed on either side of the hallway, as in the Wilson House; here, too, an older kitchen wing extends from the back of one of the parlors, forming an L-shaped plan. Old Drawyers Church was begun in

The David Wilson House, Odessa, Delaware (*circa* 1769),
now the David Wilson Mansion and the Corbit Library

The John Lewden House, Christiana, Delaware (*circa* 1770), now the home of Mrs. Howard Greene

The James Moore House near Odessa, Delaware (*circa* 1773), now the home of Mr. and Mrs. George F. Kelly

1773, and the accounts of its building are fairly complete, listing the subscriptions of the members of the congregation to the building fund, but no mention is made of an architect or carpenter.[45] The church was completed in 1776, but the interior was not finished until 1833 and an attribution to a particular carpenter is therefore difficult to make. In 1888 Scharf stated that Robert May and Company had built the church, but he offered no documentation.[46]

One more house could be added to this list of Robert May attributions, both for its style and for an interesting set of circumstances relating it to the Corbit House. The Lewden House at Christiana Bridge, now the home of Mrs. Howard Greene, has the five-bay façade, the white trim, and the shuttered doorway found in the Wilson House. The entrance door is not pedimented, but its lintel is decorated with triglyphs carved in the same robust manner as the doorway of the Wilson House. The Lewden House has a pedimented gable similar to that of Old Drawyers Church, while the plan of the first floor resembles that of the Wilson House, and the paneling is similar in character to that in the Corbit House. These coincidental similarities are reinforced, both by the fact that Christiana Bridge was a grain center and shipping community much like Cantwell's Bridge, and by the fact that John Lewden, the builder of this house, was William Corbit's first cousin and also a tanner. The Lewdens were the dominant family of the community for more than a century, successively acting as farmers, tanners, storekeepers, shipowners, and traders with far-flung commercial interests and a warehouse in Santo Domingo.[47] Thus, the Lewden House and the family that owned it enjoyed an importance in Christiana Bridge parallel to that of the Corbit House and the Corbits in Cantwell's Bridge.

The heavily traveled commercial route leading from Head of Elk to Christiana could have been the means by which the supposed carpenter-architect, Robert May, of Head of Elk, came into contact with John Lewden.[48] This house, dated 1770 by an inscribed stone in the foundation, may belong to this important group of Delaware houses that appear to be the work of one firm of carpenter-architects. Furthermore, two houses built at Head of Elk in the 1760's—Partridge Hill, which is still standing, and the Tobias Rudolph House, destroyed some years ago—show enough similarities in form and woodwork detail to the Lewden House to venture a connection between them and to add further weight to the suggestion that Robert May, the ironmaster of Head of Elk, had some acquaintance with the entire group. The suppositions concerning Old Drawyers Church, the Wilson House, the Moore House, the Lewden House, and the Elkton houses have no factual basis, but continued study of these buildings may show their relationship to be more than one of artistic similarity.

On the other hand, rather than being the work of a single architect, these houses may represent a regional form of Delaware architecture. As well as being related to one another, they have elements in common with a number of brick houses in lower New Castle and upper Kent Counties. Brick, the common building material in the towns of Wilmington and New Castle, was also used for farmhouses south of Stanton, and the typical mid-eighteenth-century house of this region can be described as a low-roofed, shallow brick house—only one room deep—with a three- or five-bay façade revealing a center hall with one room on either side. The Wilson, Moore, and Lewden Houses conform to this type.

Occasionally, Delaware farmhouses made use of the so-called "Quaker plan": a single large room extending from front to back and comprising two-thirds of the length of the house, the remaining area being divided into two approximately square rooms with corner fireplaces utilizing a single chimney. Aspendale, the house built at Downs Chapel in 1771, is an example of this type and, while different in plan, is related to the Odessa houses in certain details.[49] The modillioned cornice, cut in at the ends, is similar to those of the Wilson and Moore Houses, and the interior paneling is identical to that in some of the simpler rooms of the Corbit House. A house near Drawyers Creek, identified by Scharf as Lackford Hall, shows similar exterior cornices and fielded paneling on its corner fireplaces.[50] Two later houses—the Kensey Johns House built in New Castle in 1789-1790 (for which some of the architectural drawings remain) and Woodburn, the Hillyard-Cowgill house built in Dover in 1790—have paneled fireplace walls featuring projecting chimney breasts and pedimented overmantel frames, which, though thinner and more mannered than the woodwork in the Corbit House, are definitely in the same style.[51] The conclusion may be that the region of Delaware between New Castle and Dover can boast an attractive and vigorous style of architecture, of which the Corbit House at Odessa is without question the most beautiful and sophisticated example.

Notes to Chapter 3

1. *Pennsylvania Packet*, No. 2375, September 14, 1786 (Joseph Marriott's tanyard, Old York Road, Philadelphia).

2. Corbit Papers, Deed, David Wilson and wife to William Corbit, April 23, 1777; Ann Corbit Reese Papers, Survey of William Corbit's lot, June 9, 1777.

3. Thomas T. Waterman, *The Dwellings of Colonial America* (Chapel Hill, North Carolina, 1950), p. 92.

4. No definite date is known for this addition. William Corbit wrote to his son Pennell, October 17, 1797, about building materials, and it is possible that he was referring to the kitchen wing.

5. Delaware Archives, Inventory of William Corbit's Estate, New Castle County Inventories 1820. A transcript appears in Appendix G.

6. Historical Society of Delaware, Corbit-Higgins-Spruance Papers, "Acc^{t} of Carpenter work done for Wm Corbit by Robt May & Co taken 10 Augst 1774." A transcript appears in Appendix B.

7. Delaware Archives, Inventory of William Corbit's Estate.

8. Corbit-Higgins-Spruance Papers, Fol. 1, "List of the Residue of the Household Goods of Wm. Corbit, decd." A transcript appears in Appendix F.

9. Corbit-Higgins-Spruance Papers, "An Account . . . Expences in Building My Hous Began . . . 1772." A transcript appears in Appendix A.

10. David Wilson Mansion, Inc., "Ledger, 1766-1771," Fol. 265.

11. In the *Philadelphia Directory* for 1791, Wetherill & Sons are listed as "paint and oil merchants," and James Cresson, lumber merchant, resided at 25 South Fourth Street. A reference to Wetherill & Cresson contemporary with the build-

ing accounts has not been found, but Jeremiah Cresson advertised joiners', cabinet-makers', and chairmakers' tools in the *Pennsylvania Packet* as early as March 15, 1779. Therefore it seems reasonable to describe Wetherill & Cresson as a lumber firm.

12. George Foot, *An Address, Embracing the Early History of Delaware, and the Settlement of Its Boundaries, and of the Drawyers Congregation . . .* (Philadelphia, 1842), pp. 37-41.

13. Corbit-Higgins-Spruance Papers, "Acc[t] of Carpenter work done . . ."

14. *The Builder's Dictionary: or, Gentleman and Architect's Companion*, 2 vols. (London, 1734).

15. [Robert Adam], *The Works of Robert and James Adam, Esquires* (London, 1773), p. 5.

16. Philadelphia Contributionship for the Assurance of Houses Against Loss by Fire, *Surveys*, Book 1, 1768-94, p. 13.

17. *Sir* Roger Pratt, *The Architecture of Sir Roger Pratt*, R. T. Gunther, ed. (Oxford, 1928), p. 183.

18. Corbit Papers, Marriage Certificate of William Corbit and Mary Pennell, February 19, 1773.

19. New Castle County Wills, Book K, I, 128.

20. Delaware Archives, Tax Assessment Lists, Appoquinimink Hundred, 1777-1783.

21. *An Act to Incorporate the Carpenters' Company of the City and County of Philadelphia* (Philadelphia, 1866), pp. 78-82.

22. New Castle County Wills, Book N, I, 253.

23. Cecil County Deeds, Vol. 14, p. 85.

24. Historical Society of Pennsylvania, MSS Collection, Thomas May, "A Ledger Began in the Year of our Lord one Thousand Seven Hundred and Sixty two (1762)."

25. Cecil County Deeds, Vol. 22, p. 125; Vol. 23, p. 213; Vol. 24, p. 56.

26. J. Smith Futhey and Gilbert Cope, *History of Chester County, Pennsylvania* (Philadelphia, 1881), p. 654.

27. Fiske Kimball, "The Sources of 'Philadelphia Chippendale,'" *Pennsylvania Museum Bulletin*, XXI (June, 1926), 183-93.

28. Harold Donaldson Eberlein and Cortlandt Van Dyke Hubbard, *Portrait of a Colonial City: Philadelphia 1670-1838* (Philadelphia, 1939), p. 365.

29. Joseph Downs, *American Furniture, Queen Anne and Chippendale Periods* (New York, 1952), Plate V.

30. Eberlein and Hubbard, *loc. cit.*

31. Mrs. Thomas Potts James, *Memorial of Thomas Potts, Junior* (Cambridge, Massachusetts, 1874), pp. 122, 247.

32. Kimball, *op. cit.*, p. 185.

33. Charles E. Peterson, ed., "American Notes," *Journal of the Society of Architectural Historians*, XII (October, 1953), 28.

34. Kimball, *op. cit.*, p. 185.

35. Abraham Swan, *The British Architect: or, the Builder's Treasury of Staircases* (London, 1745), Plate L.

36. ———, *A Collection of Designs in Architecture* (London, 1757), I, Plate I.

37. ———, *British Architect*, Plate IV.

38. ———, *Designs*, II, Plate 23.

39. *Ibid.*, Plates 26, 32, 40.

40. Robert W. Shoemaker, "Christ Church, St. Peter's, and St. Paul's," *Transactions of the American Philosophical Society*, Vol. 43, Part I, p. 193.

41. Swan, *Designs*, II, Plate 21.

42. David Wilson Mansion, Inc., "Ledger, 1766-1771," Fol. 265.

43. *Ibid.*, Fols. 41, 161, 168.

44. Marie E. Windell, "James van Dyke Moore's Trip to the West, 1826-1828," *Delaware History*, IV (September, 1950), 69-104.

45. Historical Society of Delaware, photostatic copy of MS records of Old Drawyers Church.

46. J. Thomas Scharf, *History of Delaware 1609-1888*, p. 1012.

47. Clinton A. Weslager, *Delaware's Forgotten River, the Story of the Christina* (Wilmington, 1947), pp. 162-63.

48. *Ibid.*, p. 30.

49. Richard Pratt, *The Second Treasury of Early American Homes* (New York, 1954), pp. 89-91.

50. Scharf, *op. cit.*, p. 986.

51. George F. Bennett, *Early Architecture of Delaware* (Wilmington, 1932), pp. 97, 138.

Acct of Carpenter work done for Wm Corbet
by Robt May & Co taken 10 Augst 1774

		£ S D
28 Sqr 24 ft	Lathing & Shingling ... a 13/ sqr	13 . 3 .
19 sqr 40 ft	Frameing in ye Roof ... a 8/6	8 . 4 . 11
3 sqr 24 ft 5 ins	boarding on ye Terrass ... a 25/	4 . 1 . 1
2 sqr 64 ft	Frameing undr Ditto ... a 9/	1 . 3 . 9
2 sqr 64 ft	Ditto undr Ditto ... a 15/	1 . 19 . 5
	A Joice Framed across Ditto	1 . 6
	A Trap Door &c	15 .
	71 ft 8 ins Cornice & facia ... a 8d	2 . 7 . 9
	69 ft 8 ins Chineas Latice ... a 3/6	12 . 3 . 10
	32 ft 4 Ledge on ye eave a 4d 36 ft Leaden gutters a 8d	1 . 14 . 9
	2 Dormer winds in ye front a 95/ 3 Ditto back a 45/	16 . 5 .
3 sqr	29 ft Raising pieces & Wall plates ... a 10/	1 . 12 . 11
	128 ft 2 ins Cornice a 22d 332 ft Ditto a 7/6	36 . 12 . 11
	17 ft 7 ins Caseing to Door way a 3d 86 ft 3 ins Partition a 16/	18 . 4
	A Step Ladder in Garrett 12/ a small Door undr Ditto 2/	14 .
3 sqr	81 ft 9 ins Rough partition a 8/ sqr 3 Door frames a 8/	2 . 14 . 6
	53 ft 10 ins Doors a 10½ 89 ft Inside caseing a 3d	3 . 9 . 4
	30 ft Sill board & face undr 10 winds a 3d 60 Lights sashes a 7d	2 . 2 . 6
	12 Lights Gothick sashes a 3/6 & Caseing 5 winds	2 . 10 . 6
3 sqr	50 ft Ashlings a 7/ & 2 small doors in Do hung	1 . 9 . 6
	268 ft Skirting a 3¼ 12 sqr 63 ft Floor boarding a 11/ sqr	10 . 6
17 sqr	95 ft 5 ins Joices a 7/ sqr 137 ft 4 ins large Trims, Girds, &c a 5 ft	9 . 4 . 10
	Railing round head of stairs 17/4 ye Comn Stairs 15 steps 22/6	1 . 19 . 10
	80 ft 11 ins rough partition a 8/ & Strips put up for plaistering 2/	8 . 5
	135 ft 4 ins Doors & their frames &c a 10½ ft 86 ft 9 ins rabt strips a 3d	7 . . 0
	7 ft Inside caseing a 4d 3 yds 6 ft [illegible] wainst a 4/	1 . 4 . 10
	Railing about head of Stairs 10/5 35 ft 7 ins base & st base a 9d	1 . 17 . 1
1 sqr	85 ft 7 ins Closet Shelves a 24/ sqr 32 ft Jaumcaseing a 4d	1 . 16 . 7
	Lineing & hanging 2 Winds a 4/6 16 ft 7 ins Jaum caseing a 6d	17 . 3½
13 yds	8 ft 7 ins Wainst a 6/ 63 ft 10 ins Ovolo a 4d	5 . 4 . 11
	32 ft 2 ins Jaum caseing a 6d 16 ft 6 ins Ditto a 4d	1 . 1 . 7
	48 ft 2 ins Shelves [illegible] a 24/ sqr 44 ft rabt strips & Cloke rail a 3d	1 . 2 . 6½
	47 ft 3 ins Door a 10½ 42 ft 4 ins base & st base a 9d	3 . 13 . 0½
	20 ft 8 ins Cornice a 8d 31 ft 6 ins rough partition a 5/ sqr	1 . 2 . 3
	Lineing & hanging 2 Winds a 4/6 13 yds 4 ft 4 ins Wainst a 6/	4 . 9 . 10½
	48 ft 4 ins Door a 10½ 67 ft 9 ins Ovolo a 4d 18 ft 9 ins Archve a 7d	3 . 9 . 1½
	A Ground and Archve [illegible] A Mantle cornice 12/ 67 ft 8 ins Cornice a 12	4 . 3 . 8
	34 ft 10 ins Shelves [illegible]	8 . 4
	37 ft 6 ins rabt strips [illegible] 43 ft 2 ins base & st base a 9d 32 ft 8 ins Jaum caseing a 6d	2 . 18 . 1
	Beads before ye sashes & hanging 2 Winds a 3/6 16 ft 9 ins Jaum caseing a 5d	13 . 11½
	185 ft Archs Frieze & Cornice a 2/6 ft 51 yds 3 ft 8 ins wainst above ye st base with bolection moulding a 5/6 yd	36 . 13 . 3
15 yds	5 ft 3 ins Dado a 4/6 [illegible] ft 6 ins Base & st Base a frett in each a 2/6	13 . 3 . 10½
	2 Grounds undr Plaisters a 5/4 57 ft 1 ins Archs a 7d	2 . 3 . 11½
	Carried over	229 . 7 . 10½

Bill from Robert May and Company, 1774

Chapter 4

The Record

The Corbit House is one of the best-documented houses in America. The date of its erection is established; its cost is known; even the names of some of the workmen are available. The papers of the Corbit family, supplemented by religious and legal documents, have made it possible to study the life of William Corbit in relation to his house. A careful analysis of these documents has provided a surprisingly complete picture of William Corbit, his house, and the part he played in the society of his times.

The marriage certificate of William Corbit and Mary Pennell and the will of William Corbit's father have added important information to the story of the Corbit House. These papers establish the fact that Robert May—be he carpenter, architect, or contractor—was in the area of Cantwell's Bridge, but give no corroboration to the traditional designation, "Robert May of London." He could have been a Philadelphian, and it is not impossible that he was simply a gifted local carpenter. Nothing more definite is known about him, but establishing his presence in New Castle County makes it possible to describe the Corbit House as a native production rather than a British importation. It reflects some of the technical, if not cultural, independence of the American colonies on the eve of the Revolution.

The building accounts William Corbit kept reveal the importance of water transportation in the procurement of the materials for the house, and indirectly show its importance in the economy of the port community of Cantwell's Bridge. The accounts also show the slow, careful process of building in the eighteenth century, when the roof was not put on until a year after the walls had been started, and the plaster was allowed to age for months before the house was used. These records, when combined with the bill from Robert May, offer a clear picture of the construction of the house. The practice of bringing in the carpenters and other skilled craftsmen was an old one wherever a great house was to be built in the country. The carpenter's acquaintance with English design books is obvious from the designs he incorporated in the Corbit House woodwork. Certainly his knowledge of architectural terms is evident in the descriptions included in his bill, and inferences can be made as to his education from this record alone.

About William Corbit, much can be gathered from his house and papers. A man who, before his thirtieth birthday, built as fine a house as William Corbit did, must have been first of all a good businessman. Although there is no record of his having any formal education, he must have been sophisticated enough to appreciate a second-floor drawing room, even though he did use it later as a bedroom. The furniture from the house still in existence indicates that William Corbit and the wives who helped him choose it had excellent taste. This furniture, in its blending of the Philadelphia styles with Quaker plainness, illustrates a factor which is important to the interpretation of William Corbit's house. The house is imposing and beautiful, but its handsome façade and superbly carved woodwork do not connote extravagant display. William Corbit built a fine house, of the best materials and in the latest style, and he bought some furniture of superior quality, but he could hardly be considered ostentatious. This is the house of a Quaker—albeit a wealthy Quaker and one who did not always conform—and the character of the house is in keeping with the Quaker virtues of simplicity and "elegant neatness." [1] The beauty of the house is as much dependent upon its excellent proportions and the simple, pleasing forms as upon the carved ornament; in fact, the simplicity serves as a foil for the decorated cornice and entrance.

For its location in the village of Cantwell's Bridge, the Corbit House may seem extraordinary and sumptuous; but in comparison with the Philadelphia mansions after which it was apparently modeled it is restrained and simple. William Corbit himself stands somewhere between the country Quaker and such great Philadelphia merchants as James Bringhurst and Joseph Wharton. So, too, it was with his house, which stands a little more than halfway between the country houses of many Delaware landowners and the great country mansions of Mount Pleasant and Cliveden or the Philadelphia town house of Samuel Powel.

One of the most striking facts brought out in this study of the Corbit House is the constant communication between Cantwell's Bridge and Philadelphia. The physical similarity of the house to Philadelphia houses illustrates this contact immediately. Building materials brought down the river and the possibility of the carpenters' coming from Philadelphia repeat the influence of the city upon the village. In William Corbit's personal life the contact with Philadelphia was continuous; he was trained for his trade there; some of his furniture was purchased there; he lived there for eight years, and during that period there is evidence of almost weekly correspondence with the Bridge and numerous trips back and forth. Cantwell's Bridge was by no means an isolated country town, judging by the activities of its leading family.

Thus, the lives of William Corbit and his family reflect much about the entire community—economically, religiously, socially, culturally. William Corbit's house represents the activity of his life, and he in turn represents the highest position in the social and economic structure of his community. If the history of men is told by the houses in which they lived, the objects they used every day, and the records they kept, the story of the Corbit House is a chapter in the social history of America.

Note to Chapter 4

1. Sarah Fisher of Philadelphia used "elegant neatness" to describe Deborah Norris Logan in a letter to her cousin, Sarah Fisher of Duck Creek, March 30, 1782 (Corbit-Higgins-Spruance Papers, Fol. 3). The phrase seems to be an appropriate comment on the simple dignity of the Corbit House.

Old Drawyers Church near Odessa, Delaware, 1773-1776

Chapter 5

The Epilogue

When William Corbit died, seven children survived him. His eldest son, Pennell, a young widower with two small daughters, was living nearby in the brick house his father had given him. He had taken over the operation of the tannery in 1810 and was to succeed to the ownership of the Corbit House at the death of his stepmother.[1] His term as head of the family was a short one, however, for he died in 1820, before he had completed the administration of his father's estate.[2] Pennell's half brothers were also established in Cantwell's Bridge: William Fisher Corbit as a merchant; John Cowgill Corbit as a farmer on the 200-acre plantation his father had bought from Joseph Alexander; and Daniel Corbit, also as a merchant, probably working for his half brother William.[3] The two daughters, Sarah and Mary, received the income from the rental properties in Philadelphia, as well as inheriting lots on Main Street in Cantwell's Bridge.[4] Thomas, the youngest of the family, was to receive a house and store when he came of age, but he died in Philadelphia while still an apprentice.[5] Their mother, Mary Cowgill Corbit, survived her husband by nearly thirty years, living on in the mansion house until her death in 1845. By 1832, however, only two of her children were still alive.

It can be said that the Corbits married well. William Corbit and his brothers had chosen as their brides the daughters of prosperous Quaker farmers and millers. His children married into families which were distinguished socially and politically. Pennell Corbit's wife had been Mary Clark, the granddaughter of John Cook, acting-President of Delaware State in 1782 and 1783, and the daughter of John Clark of Smyrna, who was Governor from 1817 until 1820.[6] William Fisher Corbit, a high-spirited young man who wrote poetry in imitation of Sir Walter Scott and was the heir of his grandfather, Fenwick Fisher, and his uncle, Joshua Fisher, a Dover attorney, married Rhoda Davis, the daughter of a Smyrna judge.[7] John Cowgill Corbit, sent to Chester County to learn his trade, followed the pattern set by his grandfather Corbit and married one of his Brinton relations, Harriet Brinton Trimble. Before his death he served two terms as a member of the Levy Court of New Castle County.[8] His widow married Charles Tatman, the town banker.[9] Sarah Corbit married Presley Spruance, who was later United States Senator from Delaware. The youngest of the family, Daniel, married Eliza Naudain, whose ancestor, Elias Naudain, had settled prior to 1720 on a tract of land in Appoquinimink Hundred not far from the farm of the first Daniel Corbit.[10]

As his brothers died, Daniel Corbit assumed the responsibilities of the head of the family. He took over the management of the tanyard when his half brother Pennell died, and also became the guardian of his two nieces. Educated at the Friends School in Smyrna and trained for business by his half brother William, he took such an interest in the business and civic life of the community that he, like his father before him, was virtually the squire of Cantwell's Bridge. In the eyes of the townspeople he was also the town lawyer and was called upon to write legal documents, to serve as executor of estates, and to run the post office. Before his twenty-fifth birthday, he ran unsuccessfully for the Levy Court, but he later served in the State Legislature, was a member of the Constitutional Convention in 1852, and was several times proposed for Governor. In business, Daniel Corbit gave up the operation of the tanyard in the 1850's when the supply of tanbark diminished and the larger tanneries in Wilmington came into prominence. He then turned to agriculture, adding to the acreage he had inherited and improving all the farms he owned. He was among the first in Appoquinimink Hundred to set out peach orchards and realized a substantial profit from the peach yield before the blight set in, as it had earlier in Red Lion and St. Georges Hundreds to the north. A biographer said of Daniel Corbit: "All his manner and appearance indicated the native nobility of his nature, and impressed all who met him. He was very benevolent, and as a strict Friend, might be chosen as a representative of the highest type of that order of Christians." [11] This patriarch died in 1877.

It is significant to this study that Daniel Corbit took a keen interest in the history of his family, an attitude not often associated with nineteenth-century businessmen. After the death of his first wife, he married his cousin, Mary Corbit Wilson, the granddaughter of David Wilson and Mary Corbit, thus uniting the Wilsons and the Corbits once again. He gathered together many of the family papers still in existence, a majority of them bearing annotations or identifying titles in his handwriting. Conscious of the importance of the mansion house his father had built, Daniel Corbit attempted to keep its furniture intact. He bought from his sister, Sarah Corbit Spruance, most of her share, and bought in from his brother Pennell's heirs the clock, desk and bookcase, and books that had been willed to them. This family interest and the pattern of responsibility he passed on to his youngest son, Daniel Wheeler Corbit.

Like his father, the younger Daniel was educated at Quaker schools and was then sent to Haverford College. He devoted himself to managing the family farms and took part in the business life of the village, which since 1855 had borne the name Odessa (in honor of the Ukranian grain port it expected some day to rival). He served as president of the New Castle County National Bank across the street from his house, and as president of both the Cantwell Mutual Fire Insurance Company and the Odessa Loan Association. In addition, he served as a trustee of Delaware College and later of the University of Delaware. In 1870, Daniel W. Corbit married his Presbyterian cousin, Mary Clark Higgins, granddaughter of his uncle, Pennell Corbit, and in later life was himself a Presbyterian and an elder of Drawyers Church.[12]

With the death of Daniel Wheeler Corbit in 1922, the male line of William Corbit's family ended. In his lifetime, he had seen the town of Odessa change from a bustling shipping center that annually sent 400,000 bushels of wheat northward, to a quiet country village. When the Delaware Railroad was laid four miles to the west, the farmers deserted the waterway and took their produce to the railroad platform at Middletown for transport to the city. The wharves at Odessa decayed and the granaries fell down; a cannery took their place. Only the steamer "Clio," a vestige of former glory, continued to make its weekly trips to Philadelphia.

Daniel Wheeler Corbit had no son to take over his house and farms. His daughters, Sara Corbit Levis and Louise Corbit Duer, took the furniture to their homes in Wilmington, where it remains in the possession of their heirs. The life of the Corbits in the Corbit House had come to an end. In 1938 the property was sold to H. Rodney Sharp, who had come to know Odessa when he taught school there shortly after 1900 and who had visited "Mr. Dan" Corbit in the big house at the end of the street. It was Mr. Sharp's intention to restore the Corbit House, furnish it with eighteenth-century furniture, and preserve it as a small private museum.

The restoration of the house was a careful and accurate procedure, facilitated by the circumstances of the house—very few changes had been made in the original fabric, and, in addition, the Robert May bill provided a key for the identification of the original woodwork. During the ownership of Daniel Wheeler Corbit, certain modernizations had taken place to suit the changing tastes of the late nineteenth century. A porch had been added to the back of the house, and windows opening onto it had been cut to floor length. A two-story bay window punctured the solid north wall, and a wooden stair tower had been attached to the south wall to carry the service stairs to the third floor. Inside, the wall between the parlor and William Corbit's downstairs bedroom had been opened on either side of the fireplace to permit circulation between the two rooms. A colonial-style mantel had been applied over the paneling in the rear room, apparently to make the fireplace more imposing. Fortunately the paneling that had been removed had been stored in the barn, and this was now replaced. Part of an iron fireback was being used as the step of an outbuilding; it too was replaced in the fireplace from which it had been removed.[13] The paints were scraped to determine the original colors of the woodwork; these have been reproduced in most of the rooms. The inventory of William Corbit's estate, while not followed precisely in the furnishing of the house, was used as a guide, and an effort was made to include in the house furniture from an area within a hundred miles of Odessa.

Although the Corbit House had always been a private home, its architectural importance was widely known; and, after its restoration, interest in it increased markedly. On "Odessa Days," when the distinguished buildings in the vicinity were opened to the public, the Corbit House was a center of interest. Published articles had made the house familiar to students of architectural history, and the concern for the permanent preservation of the house steadily increased because of its architectural quality and because of the role it had played in the social history of Delaware. In 1958 H. Rodney Sharp presented the Corbit House to the Winterthur Corporation to maintain as a house museum and to develop an educational program centered around it. It is expected that The Henry Francis du Pont Winterthur Museum and the University of Delaware will work jointly in the development of this project, as the two institutions have in the operation of the Winterthur Program in Early American Culture. Thus the Corbit House will provide for future generations a picture of eighteenth-century Delaware life and will form a focal point for the study of that subject.

The house now appears much as it did when William Corbit, tanner and landholder, completed it. The land between the house and the Creek had been acquired and landscaped and the buildings on it restored, so that the house now has a setting in keeping with its dignity and importance, giving to the entire east end of the town the appearance of an eighteenth-century village. Today, the pride of Odessa is the Corbit House which, with the buildings around it, stands a monument to American architectural and social history. This handsome house in a country town, reflecting as it does the economic and social life of colonial Americans, as well as their architectural tastes and aspirations, does indeed bring grandeur to the banks of the Appoquinimink.

Notes to Chapter 5

1. Corbit-Higgins-Spruance Papers, Will of William Corbit.

2. Corbit family Bible.

3. Corbit-Higgins-Spruance Papers, Will of William Corbit.

4. *Ibid.*

5. *Ibid.;* Friends Historical Library, Hinshaw Index, Philadelphia Monthly Meeting.

6. Henry C. Conrad, *History of the State of Delaware* (Wilmington, 1908), p. 832.

7. Corbit-Higgins-Spruance Papers, Fol. 4, Autobiographical Notes, William Fisher Corbit.

8. J. Thomas Scharf, *History of Delaware 1609-1888*, p. 529.

9. *Ibid.*, p. 1010.

10. *Ibid.*, p. 1016.

11. J. M. McCarter and B. F. Jackson, eds., *Historical and Biographical Encyclopedia of Delaware* (Wilmington, 1882), p. 371.

12. *Ibid.*, p. 372.

13. MS notes in the possession of H. Rodney Sharp.

Appendix A

William Corbit's Building Accounts [1]

An Account [. . .] Expences in Building My Hous Began [. . .] 1772		£	S	D
	To 89250 Bricks pr [Nicholas Sellers] At 20/ pr Thousand	89	2	6
	To Laying Do By Jacob [. . .] 3/ pr Thousand	57	19	4
	To Laying 109 Perch of Stone [in] Seller At 3/9 pr perch	20	8	9
	To 40 Hhd. of Lime Some At 22/6 and Some At 22/	45	0	0
	To Stone from Chester	3	0	0
	To halling the Whole Stone for Seller	7	2	6
	To One hand helping Load Do	2	15	0
1772	To Window Arches and facia pr Stone Cutters Bill	22	17	1
July 14	To 1000 foot 5/4 pine Boards	8	0	0
	To 500 foot Ceder 500 Do pine Inch of Wetheral & Cresson	4	15	0
	To Boards pr John Bryans	3	19	11
	To Do pr John Bryans	2	8	6

1. Transcript of the manuscript in the Historical Society of Delaware, Corbit-Higgins-Spruance Papers.

		£	S	D
	To D° I got of Jer^{m} Cresson	3	0	0
	To 1000 foot of Ceder	5	0	0
	To portrage	0	2	6
	To 1000 foot 5/4 pine Bords 559 Inch D° 280 Two Inch 100 foot 3 Inch p^{r} David Van Dyke	13	2	10
	To 2011 feet 5/4 pine of D°	14	1	6
	To 2112 foot of Inch D° of D°	8	9	6
	To 2000 foot of Inch D° of D°	8	0	0
	To Bords p^{r} Nicolas Sellers	2	0	0
	To Lead for Dormants	5	0	0
	To 1 Cask of Nails p^{r} John Bryans	8	18	9
1773	To 6600 Shingles At 4:10:0 p^{r} Thousand Including Dressing	29	14	0
Ap^{r} 29	To Ceder 1800 feet 1020 foot pine 650 feet Inch & q^{tr} With Freight &c Amounts to	21	10	0
	Sprigs 12/ 205 Lights of Glass 9 by 11½ (£ S D) 9:7:11	9	19	11
	To 2 Boxes of Glass 8 by 10 At (£ S D) 3:15:0 p^{r} Box	7	10	0
	To Lead for flat of Roof	3	0	0
May 12	To 120 Qts of White lead at 9½^{d} 8 gallons oyl 3/4 hundred Whiting & other paints as p^{r} Bill	8	14	4
June 10	To Lead Whiting &c As p^{r} Bill	2	0	0
	To Oyl for Roof [...]	2	15	0
	To 1619 feet Boards [...]	12	19	13
30	To Cash paid [...] glasing & painting	10	3	0
	Boarding for D° [...]	2	2	6
		445	11	8

		£	S	D
1773 *August 14th*	To 628 foot [. . .] 14/	4	7	11
	To 1000 D^{o} [. . .] Carting hole	5	14	11
30	To 1000 Ceder [. . .]	4	15	0
	To 6 Hhd Lim [. . . at 19/] & freight	7	1	0
	Carterage	0	9	0
Oct 15	To 6 D^{o} at 18/ & freight	6	15	0
	To 2 D^{o} at 19/ & freight	2	7	0
De^{c} 29	To plastering in part Don[e] p^{r} Bill	30	8	6
	To Laths Splitting &c	6	10	0
	To Bricks	1	15	0
	To freight p^{r} I^{s} Starr	0	10	0
	To the Whole Bill of Scantling	58	9	0
1774	To Cleening Seller	1	15	0
	To 504 foot Boards Inch 200 Inch & qt^{r}	4	3	6
	To halling D^{o}	0	15	0
	To Turning Done p^{r} Bill	1	18	9
	To 131 foot two Inch plank To 96 foot Inch D^{o} At Meeting hous	2	0	6
	To 400 foot Boards p^{r} Jessy	2	0	0
	To Stone Cutters bill for front Door	21	8	9
	To Bords of Wm Walker & Ab^{r} Vandike	2	17	6
	To D^{o} Bords of Davin V^{an}Dyke Inch 400	7	5	10
	Inch qt^{r} 664	1	0	0
	To bricks of Sa^{m} Floyd 1500	2	5	0

		£	S	D
	To Stone from Chester to put on Wall	2	5	0
	Do from [Sharps]	3	15	0
	To 3 Hd[s] lime at 18/	2	14	0
	To lead for Windows Cord &c	6	9	11½
	To 4000 -/6 Nails of Sa[m] Young	1	14	0
	To Oyl & Whitelead & paints p[r] Stride	13	9	0
	To 9 Hhd[s] of lime at 23/6 for plast[r]	10	11	6
	To 60 [lbs lath nails] of Derrough	3	10	0
	To Sundry [Nails . . .] at Derroughs	12	10	0
	To [Stackhouse . . .] finishing Gla[s]	17	0	8
	To part of [. . .] nside p[r] Stride	6	0	6
	To Bord [. . .]	1	10	0
	To 6000 [laths . . . p]lastering	3	0	0
	To 28 Bushel [. . .] at 1/3 p[r] Bushel	1	15	0
		£262	8	9
	To hinges Screws [. . . at] Wilmington	1	15	0
	To Cash paid [. . .] Iron Work	9	2	6
	To D[o] p[d] John [. . .] Roof Spikes &c	8	17	6
	To James Bringhur[st. . .] for locks & hinges	13	1	15
July 20	To Dickson & Millins [. . .] for Nails locks	13	9	6
	Screws & hinges &c [. . .] a former bill	7	18	9
	To Richard Lippincots bilding An oven turning trimers Walling About Windows Steps & Wall &c	10	0	0
	To Da[d] Wilsons Acc[t] for Nails &c	15	0	9
	To halling Bricks at 2/6 p[r] Thousand	11	10	0

		£	S	D
	To Sand at River having D° All	16	10	0
	To Freight As p^r Thos Starrs Acct To halling boards lime &c Stone from landing	6	0	0
	To the Whole bill of Carpenters Work Measureing Included	543	7	6
1775 *De^c*	To Cash paid Jo^s Stride for painting	13	1	7
	To boarding D°	3	15	0
	To Iron back & Jaums p^r Da^d Wilson	5	7	6
		£678	15	0

£	S	D	
445	11	0	
250	6	9	
638	12	16	
40	0	0	Am^t not in
1374	11	9	

Appendix B

Bill of Robert May and Company [1]

Acc^{t} of Carpenter work done for Wm Corbit
by Robt May & Co taken 10 Augst 1774

			£	S	D
20 Sq^{r}	24 f^{t} Lathing & Shingling	at[2] 13/sq^{r}	13	3	0
19 sq^{r}	40 f^{t} Frameing in ye Roof	at 8/6	8	4	11
3 sq^{r}	24 f^{t} 5 in^{s} boarding on ye Terrass	at 25/	4	1	1
2 sq^{r}	64 f^{t} Frameing und^{r} Ditto	at 9/	1	3	9
2 sq^{r}	64 f^{t} Ditto und^{r} Ditto	at 15/	1	19	5
	A Joice Framed across Ditto		0	1	6
	A Trap Door &c		0	15	0
	71 f^{t} 8 in^{s} Cornice & facia	at 8^{d}	2	7	9
	69 f^{t} 8 in^{s} Chineas Lattis	at 3/6	12	3	10
	32 f^{t} 4 Ledge on ye eave at 4^{d}	36 f^{t} Leader gutters at 8^{d}	1	14	9

1. Transcript of the manuscript in the Historical Society of Delaware, Corbit-Higgins-Spruance Papers.
2. The word "at" has been substituted throughout for "a" used in the manuscript.

		£	S	D
	2 Dormer win^{ds} in ye front at 95/ 3 Ditto back at 45/	16	5	0
3 sq^{r}	29 f^{t} Raising pieces & Wall plates at 10/	1	12	11
	128 f^{t} 2 in^{s} Cornice at 22^{d} 332 f^{t} Ditto at 1/6	36	12	11
	17 f^{t} 7 in^{s} Caseing to Doorway at 3^{d} 86 f^{t} 3 in^{s} Partition at 16/	0	18	4
	A Step Ladder in Garrett 12/ a small Door und^{r} Ditto 2/	0	14	0
3 sq^{r}	81 f^{t} 9 in^{s} Rough partition at 8/ sq^{r} 3 Door frames at 8/	2	14	6
	53 f^{t} 10 in^{s} Doors at 10½ 89 f^{t} Quoine caseings at 3^{d}	3	9	4
	30 f^{t} Sill board & face und^{r} to wind^{s} at 3^{d} 60 Lights sashes at 7^{d}	2	2	6
	12 Lights Gothick sashes at 3/6 & Caseing 5 wind^{s}	2	10	6
3 sq^{r}	50 f^{t} Ashlings at 7/ & 2 small doors in D^{o} hung	1	9	6
	268 f^{t} Skirting at 3^{d} f^{t} 12 sq^{r} 63 f^{t} Floorboarding at 11/ sq^{r}	10	6	0
17 sq^{r}	95 f^{t} 5 in^{s} Joices at 7/ sq^{r} 137 f^{t} 4 in^{s} large Trim^{r}, Gird^{s}, &c at 5^{d} f^{t}	9	4	10
	Railing around head of stairs 17/4 & Com^{n} Stairs 15 steps 22/6	1	19	10
	80 f^{t} 11 in^{s} rough partition at 8/ & Strips put up for plaistering 2/	0	8	5
	135 f^{t} 4 in^{s} Doors & their frames &c at 10^{d} ½ f^{t} 86 f^{t} 9 in^{s} rab^{t} strips at 3^{d}	7	0	0
	7 f^{t} Quoine caseing at 4^{d} 3 y^{ds} 6 f^{t} 9 in^{s} wains^{ct} at 4/	1	4	10

		£	S	D
	Railing about head of Stairs 10/5 35 f^{t} 7 in^{s} base & s^{r} base at 9^{d}	1	17	1
1 sq^{r}	8 f^{t} 7 in^{s} Closet Shelves at 24/ sq^{r} 32 f^{t} Jaum caseing at 4^{d}	1	16	7
	Lineing & hanging 2 Win^{ds} at 4/6 16 f^{t} 7 in^{s} Jaum caseing at 6^{d}	0	17	3½
13 y^{ds}	8 f^{t} 7 in^{s} Wains^{ct} at 6/ 63 f^{t} 10 in^{s} Ovolo at 4^{d}	5	4	11
	32 f^{t} 2 in^{s} Jaum caseing at 6^{d} 16 f^{t} 6 in^{s} Ditto at 4^{d}	1	1	7
	48 f^{t} 2 in^{s} Shelves at 24/ sq^{r} 44 f^{t} rab^{t} strips & Cloke rail at 3^{d}	1	2	6½
	47 f^{t} 3 in^{s} Door at 10½ 42 f^{t} 4 in^{s} base & s^{r} base at 9^{d}	3	13	0¾
	20 f^{t} 8 in^{s} Cornice at 12^{d} 31 f^{t} 6 in^{s} rough partition at 5/ sq^{r}	1	2	3
	Lineing & hanging 2 Wind^{s} at 4/16 13 y^{ds} 4 f^{t} 4 in^{s} Wains^{ct} at 6/	4	9	10½
	48 f^{t} 4 in^{s} Door at 10^{d}½ 47 f^{t} 9 in^{s} Ovolo at 4^{d} 18 f^{t} 9 in^{s} Arch^{ve} at 7^{d}	3	9	1½
	A Ground und^{r} Arch^{ve} A Mantle cornice 12/ 67 f^{t} 8 in^{s} Cornice at 12^{d}	4	3	8
	34 f^{t} 10 in^{s} Shelves at 26/ sq^{r}	0	8	4
	37 f^{t} 6 in^{s} rab^{t} strips at 3^{d} 43 f^{t} 2 in^{s} base & s^{r} base at 9^{d} 32 f^{t} 8 in^{s} Jaum caseing at 6^{d}	2	18	1
	Beads before ye sashes & hanging 2 Wind^{s} at 3/6 16 f^{t} 9 in^{s} Jaum caseing at 5^{d}	0	13	11¾
	185 f^{t} Arch^{v} Frieze & Cornice at 2/6 f^{t} 51 y^{ds} 3 f^{t} 8 in^{s} wains^{ct} above ye s^{r} base with bolection moulding at 5/6 y^{d}	36	13	3

		£	S	D
15 yds	5 ft 3 ins Dado at 4/6 76 ft 6 ins Base & sr base a frett in each at 2/6	13	3	10½
	2 Grounds undr Pilasters at 5/4 57 ft 1 in. Archv at 7d	2	3	11½
	Carried over	229	7	10½
	Amt brot forwd	£229	7	10½
	6 Knees to Archv at 1/8 16 ft 5 ins Jaum caseing at 5d	0	16	10
	47 ft 3 ins Jaum caseing at 5d 54 ft small Ovolo at 3d	1	13	2
	6 Knees to ye Ovolo at 8d 40 ft 5 ins Double Door at 1/4	2	17	10
	19 ft 11 ins Door at 10d 49 ft 10 ins fluted Pilasters at 2/6	7	1	2
	6 ft 6 ins Caps to Pilasters at 3/ 1 Pedimt 55/	3	14	6
	A Tabernacle frame 15/ Mantle cornice &c 35/	2	10	0
	13 ft 8 ins Ovolo & 2 Knees 6/3 3 Pedimts at £3	9	6	3
	Beading & hanging 3 winds at 3/6 6 sqr 44 ft partition of scantling at 6/ sqr	2	9	2
	93 ft 6 ins strips put up ye wall for plaistering	0	11	8½
	A bordr round fireplace 3/6 14 sqr 25 ft Joices &c at 8/ sqr	5	17	6
13 sqr	23 ft Floor boarding at 15/ sqr	9	18	5½
	52 ft 5 ins Modillion cornice at 2/6 57 ft Archv at 7d	8	4	3½
	6 Knees to Archvs at 1/8	0	10	0
1 yd	7 Wainsct at 6/6 8 ft 9 ins Pedestal mouldings at 13d	1	1	0¾
	Lineing and hanging 1 Wind 4/ 14 ft 5 ins Jaum caseing at 4d	0	8	9¾

		£	S	D
	16 f^{t} single Arch^{v} at 5^{d} 39 f^{t} 10 in^{s} Doors at 12^{d}	2	6	6
	Com^{n} Stairs 15 Steps 3 f^{t} going 23/9 102 f^{t} 10 in^{s} Doors with their frames &^{c} at 10^{d}	5	9	5
	9 f^{t} 4 in^{s} Quoine caseing at 3^{d} 55 f^{t} 3 in^{s} rough partition 4/7¼	0	6	11¼
1 sq^{r}	40 f^{t} 8 in^{s} Newel board & shelves &c at 24/sq^{r} 65 f^{t} rab^{t} strips at 3^{d}	2	9	10
6 y^{ds}	5 f^{t} 1 in. Wains^{ct} at 5/6 16 f^{t} 9 in^{s} Cornice & broad facia at 7^{d} f^{t}	2	5	7¾
	7 Steps 3 ft 4 in^{s} going 11/1 41 f^{t} 2 in^{s} base & s^{r} base at 9^{d}	2	1	11½
	Strips put up for plaistering 1/ 41 f^{t} 6 in^{s} Jaum caseing at 4^{d}	0	14	10
	Lineing & hanging 3 Win^{ds} at [. . .] 14 f^{t} Jaum caseing at 8^{d}	1	1	4
13 y^{ds}	6 f^{t} 10 in^{s} Wains^{ct} at 5/6 16 f^{t} 10 in^{s} Cornice at 12^{d}	4	12	7¼
	46 f^{t} 8 in^{s} Ovolo at 4^{d} 35 f^{t} 7 in^{s} Doors at 10^{d}	2	5	2½
	53 f^{t} 10 in^{s} rab^{t} strips & Cloak rail at 3^{d} 36 f^{t} Shelves at 3^{d}	1	2	5½
	3 Scallopt Shelves at 3/4 18 f^{t} 7 in^{s} Arch^{v} at 8^{d}	1	2	4½
	16 f^{t} 7 in^{s} Jaum caseing at 9^{d} 46 f^{t} base & s^{r} base at 9^{d}	2	2	5¼
	32 f^{t} 4 in^{s} Jaum caseing at 6^{d} Hanging & Lineing 2 Win^{ds} at 4/6	1	5	2
13 y^{ds}	6 f^{t} 9 in^{s} Wains^{ct} at 6/6 47 f^{t} 9 in^{s} Ovolo at 4^{d}	5	5	3½
	2 Knees to Ovolo 2/ 20 f^{t} Door at 1/ f^{t} 20 f^{t} Door at 1/3	2	7	0

		£	S	D
	23 f^{t} Shelves at 3^{d}	0	5	9
	3 Shelves scallopt at 3/4 A Tabernacle frame 5/	1	15	0
	A Mantle cornice 32/6 80 f^{t} 9 in^{s} Dentle cornice at 2/0	9	14	0
	19 f^{t} 7 in^{s} Arch^{v} at 7^{d} 2 knees to Ditto at 1/8 & a Ground to D^{o} 4/6	0	19	3
	42 f^{t} 10 in^{s} base & s^{r} base at 9^{d} a slideing shelf to Closet 7/6	1	19	7
	16 f^{t} 10 in^{s} Jaum caseing at 9^{d} 40 f^{t} single Arch^{v} at 5½	1	11	9
	4 Knees to Arch^{vs} 6/ 35 f^{t} 8 in^{s} Jaum caseing at 5^{d}	1	0	11
	Beading & hanging 2 Win^{ds} at 4/ 29 y^{ds} 1 f^{t} 6 in^{s} Wains^{ct} at 6/6	9	17	7
	63 f^{t} 8 in^{s} Pedestal moulding at 1/1 12 f^{t} 9 in^{s} Ovolo 2 Knees 6/	3	14	11¼
	Bord^{r} round hearth 3/ A mantle cornice 37/6 Taber^{cle} frame 25/	3	5	6
	19 f^{t} 7 in^{s} Arch^{v} at 7^{d} 2 Knees to Ditto at 1/8 Ground und^{r} D^{o} 4/6	0	19	3
	16 f^{t} 10 in^{s} Jaum caseing at 9^{d} one open pediment 50/	3	2	7
	84 f^{t} 8 in^{s} Dentle cornice at 2/1 40 f^{t} single Arch^{v} at 5½^{d}	9	14	8½
	4 Knees to Arch^{v} 6/ 35 f^{t} 8 in^{s} Jaum caseing at 5^{d}	1	0	11
	Beading & hanging 2 Win^{ds} at 4/	0	8	0
3 sq^{r}	77 f^{t} 9 in^{s} strips fix'd to ye walls for plaistering to 8/	1	10	2½
	Carried over	£374	7	6½

		£	S	D
	Am^{t} bro^{t} forw^{d}	£374	7	6½
9 y^{ds}	4 f^{t} 3 in^{s} Wains^{ct} at 6/6 46 f^{t} 3 in^{s} Pedestal mouldings at 1/1	5	11	7¼
	58 f^{t} 6 in^{s} Arch^{v} at 7^{d} 6 knees to Ditto at 1/8 3 Grounds und^{r} D^{o} 13/6	2	17	4
	33 f^{t} Fluted Pilasters at 2/6 8 f^{t} 8 in^{s} Base & Caps to Ditto at 2/9	5	6	4
	2 Grounds und^{r} pilasters 8/ 21 f^{t} 9 in^{s} Frieze, Arch^{v} &c at 2/3	2	16	11¼
	7 f^{t} 5 in^{s} Soffit at 9^{d} 78 f^{t} 7 in^{s} Cornice with mutules at 2/10	11	8	2½
	2 Pedim^{ts} with their Frieze at 50/ 16 f^{t} 2 in^{s} Ovolo at 4^{d}	5	5	4½
	19 f^{t} 2 in^{s} Door at 14^{d} 15 f^{t} 3 in^{s} Jaum caseing at 10^{d}	1	15	2
	18 f^{t} large Single Arch^{v} at 6^{d} 2 Knees to D^{o} 3/4	0	12	4
	18 f^{t} 11 in^{s} Door at 11^{d} 17 f^{t} 8 in^{s} skew Wains^{ct} at 14^{d}	1	17	11½
15 sq^{r}	19 f^{t} 7 in^{s} Joices at 7/ 5 sq^{r} 36 f^{t} 6 in^{s} Dowelled floor at 34/ sq^{r}	15	19	2
7 sq^{r}	47 f^{t} 2 in^{s} floor boarding at 20/ sq^{r} 26 f^{t} 10 in^{s} Door at 1/5 f^{t}	9	7	5
	15 f^{t} 8 in^{s} Large Arch^{v} at 9^{d} 7 f^{t} Circular D^{o} at 2/ & a large key stone 2/6 3 f^{t} 8 in^{s} faceing on Transum at 6^{d}	1	10	1
	9 Lights Gothic sashes at 3/9 Frontispiece with Jaum caseing, impost circular Soffit &c £18	19	13	9
	Principle stairs in ye Entry £35 59 f^{t} 9 in^{s} Dresser & closet shelves	35	14	4

		£	S	D
	A small door & frame 6/ 14 f^{t} rab^{t} strips at 3^{d}	0	9	6
	37 f^{t} Door at 10½ 30 f^{t} 11 in^{s} Jaum caseing at 9^{d} 14 f^{t} 11 in^{s} Arch^{v} at 5½	3	2	4
	small strip top Arch^{v} 1/ 25 f^{t} 4 in^{s} Jaum caseing at 4^{d}	0	9	5
	Lineing & hanging 2 Win^{ds} 7/ 15 f^{t} 9 in^{s} s^{r} base at 5^{d}	0	13	3
	48 f^{t} rough partition 2/6 Cellar Stairs 29/6 50 f^{t} plain'd partition 6/	1	18	0
	Base & s^{r} base 2/11 Lineing a win^{dw} 1/6 17 f^{t} 3 in^{s} rab^{t} strips 4/6½	0	8	11½
	hanging 5 sashes with hinges & buttons to D^{o} 3/9 2 Doors in Cellar at 9/	1	1	9
	2 Doors in Cellar at 7/6 Outside Cellar Doors & frame 17/6	1	12	6
	62 f^{t} 2 in^{s} Pallisade fence at 2/6 A pair circular Gates to Ditto 25/	9	0	5
1 sq^{r}	89 f^{t} Lintles &^{c} at 10/ 63 f^{t} 1 in^{s} Double door at 16^{d}	5	3	0¼
	302 Lights Sashes 8 by 10 at 7^{d} 196 D^{o} 9 by 11½ at 10^{d}	16	19	6
	91 f^{t} 4 in^{s} Win^{d} frame at 10^{d} 103 f^{t} 4 in^{s} Ditto at 8½^{d}	7	9	3¼
	9 Moulding sills to Ditto at 2/6 227 f^{t} 10 in^{s} Com^{n} Win^{d} frame at 6^{d}	6	16	5
	5 Win^{d} frames with bars at 7/ 13 f^{t} 4 in^{s} Ditto at 5^{d}	2	0	6¼
	36 f^{t} 5 in^{s} Shutters at 13^{d} 66 f^{t} 8 in^{s} Ditto at 15^{d} 92 f^{t} 2 in^{s} D^{o} at 16^{d}	12	5	7
	Whole amount	£563	14	0

Appendix C

Deed for the Corbit House Site[1]

Deed of David Wilson to William Corbit for 46 Perches of Land
in St. Georges Hundred

THIS INDENTURE made this Twenty third Day of April in the Year of our Lord One Thousand seven hundred & seventy seven, Between David Wilson of Saint Georges Hundred in the County of NewCastle on Delaware of the One part, And William Corbit of the Hundred & County aforesaid of the Other part, WHEREAS Hilent Benson & Jannet his Wife By sundry Good Assurances in the Law, became Siezed in their Desmesne, as in Fee, of One Moiety of a Tract of Land Situate near Cantwells Bridge in the Hundred & County aforesaid And being so seized did sell & Convey unto David Wilson, one of the Parties to these Presents, Two several Lots or parcels of Land being part of the af^{sd} Moiety, As by their Indenture duly Executed bearing Date the Twelfth day of March, One Thousand seven Hundred & sixty seven And Recorded in the Rolls Office at NewCastle in Book Y. page 383 &c. Reference thereunto had may Fully and at large appear, Now KNOW YE that the af^{sd} David Wilson for & in Consideration of the Sum of Forty Pounds current Money of the Government of the Counties of NewCastle, Kent & Sussex, on Delaware, to him in hand paid the Receipt whereof he doth hereby acknowledge & thereof doth acquit & discharge the af^{sd} William Corbit his Heirs, & Assigns, Hath granted, bargained & sold & by these Presents Doth grant, bargain, & sell, alien, release, enfeoff & confirm, to the af^{sd} William Corbit his Heirs & Assigns, a certain Piece or parcel of Land including a Lott before conveyed by the Parties to these Presents, As by Indenture Dated the 16th Day of February 1771 may more fully & at large appear, & being a part of the first mentioned Lotts

---

1. Transcript of original document in the Corbit Papers.

being Bounded as follows to wit, Beginning in the Road leading to the Landing & Tan Yard at Twenty Two feet Distance from the Eastermost corner of William Corbits Brick Dwelling House & in a line with the North Eastermost end thereof from thence with s^{d} Road South forty one Degrees West nine perches fourteen Links to a Corner stone thence North fifty four Degrees West four perches twenty one Links to a Corner stone thence North forty one Degrees East nine Perches nineteen Links thence with the North Eastmost end of the af^{sd} Dwelling House South fifty two Degrees East four perches twenty one Links to the Beginning Containing Forty six perches of Land be the same more or less, Together with all & Singular the Edifices, Buildings, Improvements, Ways, Easements, Profits, Priveledges, Hereditaments, & Appurtenances, to the above described Piece or parcel of Land & Premises with the Appurtenances which heretofore hath not been sold, conveyed, & by some good Assurance in the Law confirmed to the s^{d} William Corbit & his Heirs in Fee Simple, & likewise the Reversions, & Remainders, Rents, Issues, & profits & all the Estate, Right, Title, Interest, Property, Claim, & Demand, whatsover of him the s^{d} David Wilson of, in, & to, the above described Piece or Parcel of Land, & Premises belonging or in anywise appertaining.

To Have & To Hold the said Lott or Parcel of Land with the Appurtenances to the s^{d} William Corbit his Heirs, & Assigns, to the only proper Use & Behooff of him the s^{d} William Corbit his Heirs & Assigns forever subject to the payment of the Quitrent due & to become due to the Chief Lord of the Fee thereof And the s^{d} David Wilson for himself, & his Heirs, doth by these Presents covenant, Promise, Grant, & Agree to & with the s^{d} William Corbit his Heirs & Assigns that he the s^{d} David Wilson shall & will at any & all Times, hereafter at the Reasonable Request, & proper Costs & Charges of the s^{d} William Corbit do & Execute & cause to be done & Executed all such further & other Acts, Deeds, & Devices, in the Law as shall be necessary or as shall be Devised Advised & required by the Council at Law of him the s^{d} William Corbit for the better securing & confirming to him the s^{d} William an Absolute Estate of Inheritance in Fee Simple of, in, & to, the hereby Granted Premises.

In Witness whereof the af^{sd} David Wilson Party to these Presents hath set his hand & Seal the Day & Year first above written.

Appendix D

Will of William Corbit [1]

I William Corbit of New Castle County State of Delaware being Old and Infirm but of Sound mind Reflecting on the uncertenty of time here and knowing all men must Die Ane in Order to dispose of what Worldly property I posess both Real and Personal which the Almighty hath blest me With I make this My last Will and Testement After my Just Debts are paid I Give and Bequethe a follows to Wit

Itum 1
I leave to my Dearly beloved Wife During Her naturel Life the Dweling House I now reside in, the Ground attached thereto, Carriage House and Half the Brick Stable, With the Lot of Ground between and Tan-Yard, Also fire Wood off the place my Son John C Corbit resides, With my Horse & Gig Two Cows and my Caulard Man Abraham Dorsey, during the time of his present Indentures, Also all the Furniture of Every Discription in said House during Her Life Said furniture to be Disposed of in Manner hereafter to be mentioned

Itum 2
I Give and Bequeath to my Beloved Son Pennell Corbit after the Deca's of my Dear Wife my manson Dwelling Hous and Garding, as far Westwardly as the Brick Stable also a Lot of Ground containing Six Acres leaden to Tan-Yard (Said Tan-Yard being conveyed to Him Already,) With a Lot of upland adjoining the State Road as far Eastward as a White Oak now Standing in Said Lot as far as a Land Drain in the Side of the Meddow thence Eastwardly a few Rods to Ditch runing in a Direct line to the Creek thence Westwardly up Appowinimink Creek to Meddow belonging to John Starr and the Causway to the lane between Doct^r^ Richd C. Dale and My Self opposit Said Oak tree as specified Above Also five

1. Transcript of original document in Delaware Archives.

and a half Acres of Wood Land Adjoining the Road leading to Saml Thomas' Landing and Lands of Said Thomas & Rich^{d} C Dale to Him and His Heirs I also leave to my Son Pennell Corbit During the Life of my Beloved Wife the House and Garden He now resides in With half the Brick Stable the Westward part of Said Stable

Itum 3
I Give and Bequeath to my beloved Son W^{m} F Corbit the Store House and Lot below the Bridge With the Ground from the Road Westward, including the Corn Crib and Twenty five feet to the northward to Said Road, Also a lot of meddow from the Road and Water coarce to the Lower Sluice thence down the Creek as far as my meddow Goes from thence to the Shore thence Eastwardly on the upland and Marsh of Saml Thomas Within two perches of a Sassafrass Standing on the rising Ground Southward in a line Where my Son John C Corbit resides to the Road now ocupied by Said Corbit thence Westwardly along Said Road to the Water coarce as Aforsaid Likewise five Acres of Woodland Adjoining that of Pennell Corbit and Saml Thomas and Doctr Rich^{d} C Dale, Said W^{m} F Corbit to pay to my Son Thomas Corbit When He arives at the age of Twenty one years Two Hundred Dollars, the Afors^{d} property to Him and His Heirs

Itom 4th
I Give and Bequeath to my Beloved Son John C Corbit the Plantation He now resides on Which I bought of Joseph Ellexander Also Eight Acres of upland to the Westward of Said line and parralel With Said line from Saml Thomas' field to Within about three Rods of a Peach tree thence Eastwardly to the aforsaid Plantation, To Him and His Heirs forever

Itom 5th
I Give and Bequeath To my Beloved Son Daniel Corbit the Store and Lot above the Bridge and back of my Son W^{m} F Corbits to John Starr' line and to the Northward of what I devised to my Son William one Hundred feet from the North line of Said Corn Crib lot to the Road Also the upland Eastward of the upland I Bequathed to Son William With the Marsh atached thereto, to the Northward, Also a peace of Meddow to the Westward of the Watercoarce and from the Road including a Small peace of upland adjoining Said Road in a Direct line Where part of a Ditch is now Dug and post and rail fence Standing to the Creek thence down the Creek to the Sluice and up the Water coarce Crossing the Road, With a peace of Meddow above opposit Doct^{r} Richd Dales Orchard to the place of begining or post and rail fence, Also five Acres of Wood Land adjoining the Northern of W^{m} F Corbits Saml Thomas and Doct^{r} Richd Dale Also a Lot of Ground fronting the Main Road Adjoining Ground of Jasper Curry Dec^{d} to the North Westward and a Lot to the South Westward to my Son W^{m} F Corbit,

To Him and His Heirs Forever–The aforsaid lots to the Westward ajoinig John Starr

Itom 6th
I Give and Bequeath to my Beloved Son Thomas Corbit after the Deceas of my Beloved Wife, the House my Son Pennell now occupies and Garden. Also the Dwelling House adjoining With the Brick Store and Garden attached thereto. With the Ground from the Road leading to the Tan-Yard including the frame Buildings from the West of the Brick Stable to the line of David Wilson for Stabling My Beloved Wife to Receive the proffits of the Brick Store and Dwelling House adjoining thereof until He arrives to the age of Twenty one years for His Mentainance Also a peace of upland in a line With the Road between Doct^{r} Rich^{d} C Dale and me as to join that I Bequeathed to My Sons Pennell and Daniel With a peace of Meddow attached thereto Northwardly to the Creek, thence up the Creek until it Intersects and joins the Meddow I have left to my Son Pennell and along the aforesaid line by the Oake Tree to the Road aforesaid Also All the Marsh & Cripple from the Bridge over the Water coarce With the upland to the Southward of Said Road adjoining Lands of Saml Thomas and John C Corbit Likewise about Six Acres of Wood land to the Northward of the Lot for Danl Corbit being the residue of Woodland To Him and His Heirs

Itom 7th
I Give and Bequeath to my Beloved Daughter Sarah Corbit my three Story Brick House With the two Wooden frames D^{o} back of the Same With the lot now inclosed Also the two Story Brick House adjoining With the Yard as far Back as now Occupied the aforesaid Houses are on Eght Street Spring Garden Philad^{a} Pen^{n} Township Philad^{a} County Also Fifty feet of Ground fronting the Main Road at Cantwells Bridge New Castle County Delaware adjoining the Southward Side of a lot I Gave my Son Pennell Corbit runing to the line of John Starr

Itom 8th
I Give and Bequeath to my Beloved Daughter Mary Corbit Three Brick two Story Houses and two frame two Story D^{o} on Eight Street Spring Garden Penn Township Philad^{a} County With the Lots atached thereto adjoining the two Brick Houses I Bequeath to my Daughter Sarah With the residue of the Ground at Cantwells Bridge between Sarah Corbit and Daniel Corbit from the Main Road to the line of John Starr

I Have Fifty Acres or thereabout of Marsh and a Small portion of upland I bought of Wm Liston Which I leave to my Son John C Corbit provided He pays to my Daughter Sarah Corbit one year after my Dec^{d} 100 Dollars and to my Daughter Mary Corbit 100 Dollars and my Son Thos Corbit 100 Dollars Should

He decline the Same my Exr[s] may Sel the Same in one year after my Deces and the Am[t] thereof to be Divided between my Daughter Sarah & Mary and My Son Tho[s] Corbit

My Personal Estate I leave as follows After the Deceas of my Beloved Wife, my Clock Desk and Book Case I leave to my Son Pennell With one third of my Books the residue of my furniture I Leave to my Daughter Sarah one fourth to my Son Daniel one fourth to my Daughter Mary one fourth to my Son Thomas one fourth of the Whole of my Furniture, as to my other Personal Estate after my Debts are Paid, I leave the Same to be equally Divided between my Beloved Wife and All my Children Without naming them

Nothwithstanding my aforsaid bequest I leave to my Beloved and Kind Ancient Friend Alis Murry Who has resided With me Many Years I Bind my aforsaid Children to pay the aforsaid Alis Murry as follows Annually Without Defalcation That is to Say, Pennell Corbit Ten Dollars W[m] F Corbit Ten Dollars John C Corbit Ten Dollars Dan[l] Corbit Ten Dollars My Daughters Sarah and Mary each Five Dollars a peace Amtg to Fifty Dollars yearly for Her Mentainance

Lastly I Nominate Constitute and appoint my Beloved Son Pennell Corbit and my Son John C Corbit to be Whole and Sole Executors of this my Last Will and Testement as Witness my Hand and Seal this Eleventh Day of the third month one Thousand Eight Hundred and Seven-teen 1817

Signed and Seal'd the Day and Date Above Writen before us as Witnesses to the aforsaid Will

Witness W[m] Corbit (*Seal*)

John Starr }
D Wilson, Jun } aff[d] Aug 13

New Castle County Ss Before me personally appeared John Starr and David Wilson Junior the two subscribing Witnesses to the above and foregoing Will who being duly affirmed did severally say that they saw William Corbit the Testator sign and seal the above and foregoing Instrument of writing and heard him publish pronounce and declare the same to be his last Will and Testament—That at the time of his so doing he was (to the best of their belief) of sound disposing mind and memory—That it was at the request of the Testator in his presence and in the presence of each other they severally subscribed their names thereto as Witnesses—In Testimony whereof I have hereunto set my hand at New Castle the 13th day of August A D 1818.

Evan Thomas Reg.

Appendix E

Minutes for the Will of Mary Cowgill Corbit [1]

Minutes of Mary Corbit (My Mother) Will as she wishes her property disposed of after her decease—as directed by her about 12 mo 1843, Viz

To My Daughter Sarah Spruance Four Hundred Dolls. in Cash—also a pair of plated Candlesticks—My Snuff Box, old family Testament—Bedstead—bed—bolsters—& pillows which I sleep on—pr. of new blankets—pr. of New linen Sheets old bed quilt I worked when young—My Gold Watch—and all My Wearing apparel—& Spectacles

To James Corbit—Twenty Dolls. in Cash

To Eliza N. Corbit—New Carpet, & oil Cloth in Back room down Stairs—fringe Notted Counterpane and "Life of Mary Dudley"—

To S C Higgins—Sett of New dark Cahes bed Curtains

To M P Naudain—Marcaiy Counterpane

To H B Corbit, Mahogany Wash Stand—pr. Cellery Glasses

To Mary C Hagg Cash Twenty Dollars

To Danl Corbit—the residue of my personal property except, that I wish the balance of Cash, should there be any after payment of the above legacies, to be equally divided between My sd Son Danl & My Sd Daughter Sarah C. Spruance

Witness My hand

Mary C Corbit

---

1. Transcript of original document in the Historical Society of Delaware, Corbit-Higgins-Spruance Papers.

Appendix F

Division of William Corbit's Furniture by Daniel Corbit and Sarah Corbit Spruance [1]

List of the Residue of the Household Goods of Wm. Corbit, decd., which belongs to his daughter Sarah C. Spruance & Danl. Corbit. 11th mo 29 1845.

Side Board	$ 10.00
Card Table	4.00
old Parlor Glass	4.00
6 Mahogany Chairs	6.00
Round Table in Parlor	4.00
Candle Stand 1$ old Sofa 6$	7.00
2 Bureaus Back room up stairs	15.00
old Andirons	1.00
Breckfast Table	4.00
2 Bureaus formerly in long Room	10.00
2 Double Coverlids Blankets etc.	8.00
Cradle 4$ " old Bureaus in Garret 3$	7.00
old Couch 1.00—old Windsor chairs 3$	4.00
3 ½ Beds—26$—	26.00
3 Looking Glasses	6.00
Bell Metal Kittle & Iron Pots	4.00
1/3d the Books	6.67
Amt. card. over	$126.67

{6 best Mahogany chairs & 2 arm chairs—
divided—each took 4 of these chairs}

Amt. brot. over $126.67

Recd. 11th mo 29, 1845 of Danl Corbit, Sixty three dolls 33⅓ cts in full for My Share being one half of the aforesaid personal property of My late Father W. Corbit, decd., as valued by the said D. Corbit and myself—the remaining half being his own Share.

Sarah C. Spruance

1. Transcript of original document in the Historical Society of Delaware, Corbit-Higgins-Spruance Papers.

Appendix G

Inventory of William Corbit's Estate[1]

An inventory of the goods and chattels of William Corbit decd, that were bequeathed to his wife Mary Corbit during her natural Life appraised by us the Subscribers this 27th day of August 1818.

In Parlour

	$	*cts*
1 Sopha	25	00
6 Mahogany chairs	12	00
6 dtto do	9	00
1 Mahogany dining table	8	00
1 dtto Card Table	5	00
1 Looking Glass	10	00
1 Waiter large Size	2	00
1 East India Carpet including Entry	10	00
2 Maps	15	00
1 Clock & Case in Dineing Room	60	00
1 desk and book Case	30	00
1 Side board	20	00
1 Mahogany dineing table	8	00
1 dtto breakfast table	6	00
1 looking glass	5	00
6 Windsor chairs	3	00
Andirons Shovel & tongs	5	50
1 Carpet & fire rug	15	00
6 Silver table Spoons	15	00
5 do tea do	1	50

1. Transcript of the manuscript in Delaware Archives, New Castle County Inventories 1820.

	$	cts
In Entry Contents of cupboard	1	50
6 Windsor chairs	5	00
1 Settee	2	00
3 arm chairs	3	00
Amt card. over	$276	50
Amot brot over & Continued	276	50

(Back room North corner)

1 highpost bedStead and Saking bottom	8	00
1 bed quilt 2 Sheets 2 pillow cases & bed	20	00
1 dressing table	1	50
1 Walnut Stand	1	50
4 old Chairs	2	00
1 Small looking glass	2	00
1 couch & mattrass	12	00
1 pr. old brass andirons		50
2 window curtains	2	00
Contents of cupboard	10	00
1 Sett large Knives & fks 3.00 2 small dtto 2.50	5	50
1 ps. rag Carpeting		50

Front Chamber East corner

1 Sash Curtain	4	00
1 Chest of Magy. drawers	15	00
1 pr. of bereaus Mahogy	25	00
6 Windsor Chairs	9	00
1 Mahog. bedstead & Saking bottom	6	00
1 bed 20$ Counterpin 4$ bolster & 2 pillay	24	00
1 looking glass	4	00

(Front Chamber South corner)

1 Walnut Beurau	5	00
1 bedstead & S. g. bottom	10	00
1 bed 25$ 1 Spread 1.50	26	50
6 pr. Rose blankets	15	00
3 ditto—2.50 1 single coverlid	5	50
1 woolen quilt 5.00	5	00

	$ cts
2 pr. fine linen Sheets	8 00
3 pillow Cases	1 50
1 pr. fine linen Sheets	4 00
3 Course ditto do	3 00
1 Muslin ditto	75
Amt card. over	$513 25
Amot. brot over & Continued	513 25
1 Single coverlid 2.50—1 ditto do 2.50	5 00
2 double ditto	22 00

(Back Chamber West corner)

1 bedStead an S. g. bottom	3 00
1 bed, bolster and pillow	12 00
2 Sheets and bed quilt	3 50
1 Servants bed & bedding	2 00

(Back Chamber North corner)

1 bedStead and S. ng bottom	5 00
1 bed and bolster	20 00
2 Muslin Sheets and 1 comfortable	4 50
2 Window curtains	1 00
1 dressing Glass	1 50
Lumber in garrett	5 00

(Back room & West corner downstairs)

Sundrys in S. room	2 00
in cellar	
1 bbl Shad & 2 hhd with herrings	5 00
Sundrys in S. cellar	3 00
ditto Kitchen including wooden ware	20 00
1 ten plate Stove in ditto	15 00
Kitchen Chamber furniture	3 00
200 lb. bacon at 15 cts. pr. lb.	30 00
Horse & Gig	40 00
2 Cows	40 00
Negro man Abraham Darrey to serve five years five months & 18 days	150 00

Books

Family Bible 2$ Fennings Geography 2 vol.	4 00
Bigland View of the World 5 Vol. 2d 3d & 4th vol. Josephus	6 50

	$	cts
Pinkertons Geography 2 Vol. 1.50 Regniers Egypt 1 vol. .50	3	50
Wilson Egypt 1 vol. 75—Jno. Griffith 1 vol. .75	1	50
Stuart View 1 vol 1$	1	00
Bartrams travels 1 vol. 1.50—mecellanious pomes 1 vol.	2	00
Amot. brot. over	924	25

Amot. Brot. over & Continued	924	25
Nickar on religion 25 Thos Chalkley 1 vol. .25		50
Universal History 9 vol. 6.75 Annual Register 3 vol	8	25
Foxs Journals 1 vol.	2	00
A lot of odd Volumes Pamphtes &c	5	00
Denon Egypt 2 vol, .50 Barrow travels 1$	2	00
Calm Observer 75—Barlow husbandry 1.00	1	75
	943	75

An Inventory of the goods and chattels of William Corbit (Decd.)
Appraised by the Subscribers the 27th day of Aug^st 1818
as property not bequeathed to his wife.

Wearing Apparrel 20 Dols. Watch 2 Dols.	22	00
1 Old Cart 5 dols. 1 old Coache 50 dols.	55	00
1 Old chair & harness	5	00
2 piggs in pen 4 dol.	4	00
1 Stack of wheat Supposed 20 bushels	35	00
1 Six plate Stove 5 dols. sundry Black smith Tools including Bellows, Anvil, &c	25	00
1 cow	16	00
	162	00

Pennell Corbit }
Jno. C. Corbit } Exrs.

whole Amount $1105 75
20

Samuel Penington
John Janvier

New Castle County SS: I hereby certify that Samuel Penington and John Janvier Appeared me the Subscriber one of the Justices of the Peace in and for said County and was duly Qualified to Appraise all the Goods and Chattles of the Estate of William Corbit decd. by on signing as witness my hand and seal this 26th day of January A. D. 1820.

Th. P. Reynolds.

Appendix H

Reconstruction of William Corbit's Library

The inventory of William Corbit's estate included the titles of twenty-two books. One of these books (the *Annual Register*) is still in existence, and copies of several of the titles are now in the Corbit House. To complete the picture, this appendix, based upon the main bibliographical sources available, presents an approximate reconstruction of the original library.[1] In this list, the inventory entry is given first, followed by a complete bibliographical entry. Allowance has been made for deviations in spelling and abbreviations of the titles in the inventory.

"Family Bible"
The Holy Bible. Oxford: W. Jackson and A. Hamilton, 1784. (This Bible is now in the possession of Mrs. D. Meredith Reese of Wilmington.)

"Fennings Geography 2 vol."
Fenning, Daniel. *A New System of Geography: or, A General Description of the World. Containing a Particular and Circumstantial Account of All the Countries, Kingdoms, and States of Europe, Asia, Africa, and America. . . . With the Birds, Beasts, Reptiles, Insects, the Various Vegetables, and Minerals, Found in Different Regions.* 2 vols. London: Printed for S. Crowder, 1764-1765. (Union Library Catalog)

"Bigland View of the World 5 Vol."
Bigland, John. *A Geographical and Historical View of the World: Exhibiting a Complete Delineation of the Natural and Artificial Features of Each Country:*

---

1. The bibliographical sources used:

The British Museum, *Catalogue of Printed Books, 1881-1900* (Ann Arbor, Michigan, 1946).

Joseph Sabin, Wilberforce Eames, and R. W. G. Vail, *Bibliotheca Americana. A Dictionary of Books Relating to America, from Its Discovery to the Present Time* (New York, 1868-1936).

Union Library Catalog at the University of Pennsylvania.

U. S. Library of Congress, *A Catalog of Books Represented by Library of Congress Printed Cards* (Ann Arbor, Michigan, 1942-1946; 1942-1947; 1948-1952).

and a Succinct Narrative of the Origin of the Different Nations, their Political Revolutions and Progress in Arts, Science, Literature, Commerce, etc. . . . With Notes, Correcting and Proving the Part which Relates to the American Continent and Islands, by Jedidiah Morse. 5 vols. Boston: Thomas B. Wait and Co., 1811. (Sabin)

"2^{d} 3^{d} & 4th vol. Josephus"
Josephus, Flavius. *The Genuine and Complete Works of Flavius Josephus . . . To which is Added . . . a Continuation of the History of the Jews . . . to the Present Time . . . by George Henry Maynard.* New York: William Durell, 1792. (Sabin)

"Pinkertons Geography 2 Vol."
Pinkerton, John. *Modern Geography. A Description of the Empires, Kingdoms, States, and Colonies . . . in All Parts of the World; Including the Most Recent Discoveries, and Political Alterations.* 2 vols. London: T. Cadell, Jun. and W. Davies, 1802. First American edition: Philadelphia: John Conrad & Co., 1804. (Sabin)

"Regniers Egypt 1 vol."
Regnier, Claude Ambroise, Corps Legislatif. Conseil des Anciens. *Discours . . . en presentant l'hommage offert par le citoyen Sonini d'un ouvrage ayant pour titre, "Voyage dans la haute et basse Egypte."* Paris: Prairial, an 7, 1799. (British Museum Catalogue)

"Wilson Egypt 1 vol."
Wilson, Robert Thomas. *History of the British Expedition to Egypt.* Philadelphia: Conrad & Co., printed by Bonsal & Niles, Wilmington, 1803. (Corbit House)

"Jno. Griffith 1 vol."
Griffith, John. *A Journal of the Life, Travels, and Labours in the Work of the Ministry of John Griffith.* London: James Phillips, 1779. American edition: Philadelphia: Joseph Crukshank, 1780. (Sabin)

"Stuart View 1 vol."
Probably: Stuart, Gilbert. *A View of Society in Europe, in Its Progress from Rudeness to Refinement: or, Inquiries Concerning the History of Law, Government, & Manners.* Dublin: Whitestone, 1778. (Union Library Catalog)

"Bartrams travels 1 vol."
Bartram, William. *Travels through North and South Carolina, Georgia, East and West Florida, the Cherokee Country, the Extensive Territories of the Mus-*

cogulges, or Creek Confederacy, and the Country of the Choctaws; Containing an Account of the Soil and Natural Productions of These Regions, Together with Observations on the Manners of the Indians. Philadelphia: Printed by James and Johnson, 1791. (Corbit House)

"mecellanious pomes 1 vol."

"Nickar on religion"

Necker, Jacques. *Of the Importance of Religious Opinions.* Trans. by Mary Wollstonecraft. London, 1788. First American edition: Philadelphia: Matthew Carey, 1791. (British Museum Catalogue)

"Thos Chalkley 1 vol."

Chalkley, Thomas. *The Journal of Thomas Chalkley. To Which is Annexed, a Collection of His Works* . . . 1 vol. New York: Printed and Sold by Samuel Wood . . . Sold also by Kimber and Conrad, Philadelphia, 1808. (Library of Congress Catalog)

"Universal History 9 vol."

Probably: *A Universal History, from the Earliest Account of Time. Compiled from Original Authors; and Illustrated with Maps, Cuts, Notes, etc. With a General Index to the Whole.* . . . 65 vols. London: Printed for T. Osborne, 1747-1768. (Library of Congress Catalog)

"Annual Register 3 vol."

Annual Register; or a View of the History, Politics, and Literature, for the Year. . . . London: Printed for J. Dodsley, 1758-1862. (Library of Congress Catalog)

Mrs. Charles Lee Reese, Jr., of Wilmington, has in her possession a copy of the *Annual Register* for 1763, inscribed "Sam. Thomas" and probably bought secondhand by William Corbit.

"Foxs Journals 1 vol."

Fox, George. *A Journal, or Historical Account of the Life, Travels, Sufferings, Christian Experiences, and Labour of Love, in the Works of the Ministry, of the Ancient, Eminent and Faithful Servant of Jesus Christ, George Fox.* 2 vols. Philadelphia: Baw & Kite, 1808. (Sabin)

"A lot of odd Volumes Pamphtes &c"

"Denon Egypt 2 vol."

Denon, Vivant. *Travels in Upper and Lower Egypt, During the Campaigns of General Bonaparte.* Trans. by E. A. Kendal. 2 vols. London: B. Crosby and Co., 1802. (Corbit House)

"Barrow travels"

Barrow, *Sir* John, *bart. Travels in China, Containing Descriptions, Observations, and Comparisons, Made and Collected in the Course of a Short Residence at the Imperial Palace of Yuen-Min-Yuen, and on a Subsequent Journey through the Country from Pekin to Canton. In Which It Is Attempted to Appreciate the Rank that This Extraordinary Empire May Be Considered to Hold in the Scale of Civilized Nations . . .* London: T. Cadell and W. Davies, 1804. First American edition: Philadelphia: W. F. M'Laughlin, 1805. (Union Library Catalog)

"Calm Observer"

The Friends Historical Library at Swarthmore College supplied the following titles from *Dictionary of Anonymous and Pseudonymous English Literature:*

The American Question: a Letter from a Calm Observer to a Noble Lord . . . London, 1812.

An Examination of the Letter Addressed to Principal Hill, on the case of Mr. Leslie; in a Letter to Its Anonymous Author. With Remarks on Mr. Stewart's Postscript, and Mr. Playfair's Pamphlet. By a Calm Observer. Edinburgh, 1806.

Letters on the Subject of the Concert of Princes, and the Dismemberment of Poland and France. (First Published in the "Morning Chronicle" between July 20, 1792 and June 25, 1793.) With Corrections and Additions by a Calm Observer. London, 1793.

"Barlow husbandry"

Probably: Varlo, Charles. *A New System of Husbandry, from Many Years of Experience, with Tables Shewing the Expence and Profit of Each Crop.* 2 vols. Philadelphia: the Author, 1785. (Corbit House)

Robert May, of Head of Elk, and Corbit's cousin, John Lewden of Christiana, were listed among the subscribers to this book.

Mrs. Charles Lee Reese, Jr., has in her possession a book not included in the inventory, but inscribed "William Corbit 1786": *The Preceptor: Containing a General Course of Education Wherein the First Principles of Polite Learning Are Laid Down in a Way Most Suitable for Trying the Genius, and Advancing the Instruction of Youth.* Vol. I. Dublin: George Faulkner, 1749. This is possibly the "one Vollum of Extracts from different authers, Selected for the improvement of youth" lent by William Corbit to his son Pennell and described in the letter quoted on page 26.

Appendix I

William Corbit's Furniture

Nearly thirty pieces of furniture which are contemporary with William Corbit and are believed to have been used in his house during his lifetime remain in the hands of his descendants. Most of this furniture was inherited with the house by the late Sara Corbit Levis from her father, Daniel Wheeler Corbit, who in turn had inherited the house and its contents in 1877 from his father, Daniel Corbit, the last surviving son of William Corbit. It is now in the possession of Mrs. Levis' heirs: Mrs. Earle R. Crowe, Mrs. Charles Lee Reese, Jr., Mrs. Willard B. Purinton, and the heirs of the late Daniel Corbit Curtis. Other pieces of furniture are owned by Mrs. Levis' granddaughter, Mrs. Samuel F. Pryor III; by Mrs. D. Meredith Reese, whose father, John Cowgill Corbit, was a great-grandson of William Corbit; and by the heirs of William Corbit Spruance, who was descended from Sarah Corbit Spruance, daughter of William Corbit. The agreement made by Mrs. Spruance and her brother Daniel Corbit concerning the disposition of their father's furniture at the death of his widow is included in Appendix F.

Just as the structure of the Corbit House reflects the architectural patterns of Philadelphia and its environs, the furniture used in the house illustrates the contact the Corbit family had with the city 50 miles away. A looking glass labeled by the Philadelphia cabinetmaker and importer John Elliott and a Windsor chair bearing the stamp of William Cox, a chairmaker who worked in Philadelphia between 1767 and 1796, attest to this fact. Corbit also patronized local craftsmen, owning a tall clock made by Duncan Beard, of Appoquinimink. While none of the Corbit furniture is known to have been made by the Cantwell's Bridge cabinetmaker, John Janvier, a chest of drawers (Plate 6) bears a close resemblance to documented Janvier pieces; and, since he was commissioned to make Corbit's coffin, it is not unlikely that he would have done other work for him. The source of the rest of the furniture is not definitely known; but stylistically it appears to have been made within the area influenced by Philadelphia styles, and it is related in general appearance and in certain details to furniture owned by other Delaware families. Most of the secondary woods are indigenous to Delaware. This group of furniture is characterized by the use of handsomely figured woods, good proportions, and conservative designs. There is a marked absence of the elaborate carving found on much Philadelphia furniture of the Chippendale period, but the simplicity of Corbit's furniture is not to be considered a measure of its quality. The looking glass for which he paid £2 12*s.* indicates that his furniture was not inexpensive, but was instead in conformance with the Quaker esthetic expressed by John Reynell when he ordered his own furniture to be "of the best sort but plain." [1]

In the following list, an attempt has been made to identify the extant furniture with entries in the inventory of William Corbit's estate (Appendix G). This appendix, which also contains illustrations of most of the furniture described herein, supplements that inventory and provides another key to Corbit's tastes, thus presenting a further aspect from which to study him as a typical eighteenth-century man.

List of the Existing Furniture of William Corbit

ARMCHAIR, beech, William and Mary style, probably English (1670-1710). [*Plate 1*]

While presumably the personal property of his widow, this chair is perhaps one of the *3 arm chairs . . . 3.00* listed in William Corbit's inventory. A Cromwellian-type chair upholstered in stained leather, it has block-and-turned front legs and sausage-turned arms. Heavy rectangular stretchers brace the legs; the rear stretcher is inscribed "EN." A brass plaque on the back of the chair replaces a leather tag once attached to the bottom of the seat, bearing these words: "Cousin John Cowgill claims a certain ancient armchair, in which formerly so tradition says sat our common ancestor, the venerable Joshua Clayton, an eminent and distinguished minister of the Society of Friends, who died near one hundred years ago—D. Corbit, 2^{d} mo 14th 1833." [2] All secondary woods are beech.

Dimensions: H. 37″ H. (seat) 17″ W. 24⅝″ D. 17½″

Owned by the heirs of Sara Corbit Levis; in the possession of Mrs. Charles Lee Reese, Jr.

ARMCHAIR, maple painted black, Pennsylvania or Delaware (1760-1800).

Perhaps one of the *3 arm chairs . . . 3.00* included in William Corbit's inventory, this armchair is a traditional type featuring a ladder back formed of five arched and shaped slats. The vase-turned front legs extend to support the arms; the front stretcher is boldly turned. At some time in the chair's history, rockers were added; the rush seat is a replacement. A brass plaque on the top slat reads, "Mary Cowgill 1791." The secondary wood is tulip.

Dimensions: H. 44″ H. (seat) 17″ W. 22¾″ D. 16½″

Owned by Mrs. D. Meredith Reese (Ann Corbit).

WINDSOR ARMCHAIR, maple, tulip, and mahogany, Pennsylvania (1780-1810). [*Plate 2*]

Presumably one of the twelve Windsor chairs included in William Corbit's inventory and the one, according to family tradition, used as a desk chair by his son Daniel Corbit, this bow-back armchair has rolled knuckles on the arms, with turned front arm supports of mahogany. The saddle seat is supported by baluster-turned legs. The chair has been refinished recently.

Dimensions: H. 36¼″ H. (seat) 16¼″ W. 21½″ D. 16″

Owned by Mrs. D. Meredith Reese (Ann Corbit).

WINDSOR ARMCHAIR, tulip and hickory painted brown, Pennsylvania or Delaware (1800-1815).

Presumably one of the twelve Windsor chairs included in William Corbit's inventory, this hoop-back chair with attached arms has bamboo turnings on the spindles of the back and on the legs. The seat has a slight saddle shape.

Dimensions: H. 37½″ H. (seat) 18⅛″ W. 21⅛″ D. 17½″

Owned by the heirs of Sara Corbit Levis; in the possession of Mrs. Charles Lee Reese, Jr.

CORNER CHAIR, American walnut, Queen Anne style, probably Delaware (1740-1760). [*Plate 3*]

Possibly included among the *4 old chairs . . . 2.00* listed with the furnishings of the first-floor bedroom in William Corbit's inventory, this commode chair has a deep scalloped skirt, solid vase-shaped splats, and turned arm supports. One cabriole leg ends in a blunt foot; the other three legs are club shaped. Modern upholstery covers the slip seat.

Dimensions: H. 33⅝″ H. (seat) 17″ W. 19″ D. 19″

Owned by the heirs of Sara Corbit Levis; in the possession of Mrs. Earle R. Crowe.

SIDE CHAIR, mahogany, Chippendale style, Philadelphia or Delaware (1770-1790). [*Plate 4*]

One of the *6 Mahogany chairs . . . 12.00* listed in William Corbit's inventory, this side chair is distinguished by a bow-shaped cresting rail and pierced splat, with carved foliage decorating the interlaced strapwork in the splat. The cabriole legs end in claw-and-ball feet, while the rear legs are stump shaped in the Philadelphia manner. The slip seat is covered in modern red damask. The secondary wood is also mahogany.

Dimensions: H. 39″ H. (seat) 18″ W. 21¼″ D. 17½″

Owned by the heirs of Sara Corbit Levis; in the possession of Mrs. Earle R. Crowe.

This chair is one of an original set of eight—six side chairs and two armchairs—which was divided between Daniel Corbit and his sister, Sarah Corbit Spruance, in 1845. (See Appendix F.) Three side chairs are in the possession of the heirs of Mrs. Levis, and the other chairs have descended in the Spruance family; one is owned by Mrs. Albert W. Morse, Jr. (Louisa Spruance), of Wilmington.

Side Chair, mahogany, Chippendale style, Philadelphia or Delaware (1770-1790). [*Plate 5*]

This chair with a bow-shaped cresting rail and pierced, interlaced splat is probably one of the *6 Mahogany chairs . . . 9.00* included in William Corbit's inventory. The seat rail is molded at the upper edge, as are the outside corners of the straight legs, which are braced by rectangular stretchers. The legs have been shortened and later restored. The secondary wood is white cedar.

Dimensions: H. 38¾″ H. (seat) 18″ W. 21″ D. 16¾″

Owned by the heirs of Sara Corbit Levis; in the possession of Mrs. Earle R. Crowe.

This chair is also one of a set. In addition to three owned by Mrs. Levis' heirs, Mrs. William C. Spruance owns one, which has been cut down to "slipper-chair" height. It descended to her late husband from his grandmother, Sarah Corbit Spruance.

Windsor Side Chair, tulip and hickory, Philadelphia (*c.* 1790).

Presumably one of the twelve Windsor chairs included in William Corbit's inventory, this hoop-back Windsor chair has a saddle-shaped seat. Bamboo turnings decorate the spindles and legs, and the underside of the seat is branded "W. Cox." [3] The chair has been cut down and recently refinished.

Dimensions: H. 35″ H. (seat) 14½″ W. 17″ D. 17″

Owned by Mrs. Samuel F. Pryor III (Sara Corbit Reese).

Chest of Drawers, mahogany, Chippendale style, probably Philadelphia (1770-1790).

The original section of this chest is composed of five tiers of drawers, the upper two tiers divided into two and three drawers, and is possibly the *chest of Magy. drawers . . . 15.00* included in William Corbit's inventory. Inset quarter columns trim the corners; the removable top is decorated with a carved fretwork frieze. Brasses are replacements, and the lower section of one drawer on straight bracket feet is a modern restoration. The secondary woods are red gum and tulip.

Dimensions: H. 58½″ W. 42½″ D. 22¼″

Owned by the heirs of Sara Corbit Levis; in the possession of Mrs. Earle R. Crowe.

CHEST OF DRAWERS, mahogany, Chippendale style, probably Delaware (1790-1800). [*Plate 6*]

Perhaps one of the *pr. of bereaus mahogy . . . 25.00* listed in William Corbit's inventory, this chest rests on high ogee-bracket feet. Four graduated drawers with cock-beaded edges are framed by inset quarter columns at the corners. The brasses have been replaced. The chest is so similar to the signed chest by John Janvier in the collection of H. Rodney Sharp and now in the Corbit House that it could be attributed to the Janvier workshop. The secondary wood is tulip.

Dimensions: H. 34¼″ W. 40½″ D. 21⅛″

Owned by the heirs of Sara Corbit Levis; in the possession of Mrs. Earle R. Crowe.

An identical chest is owned by Mrs. Paul J. Nowland (Louise Corbit Lea).

CHEST-ON-CHEST, mahogany, Chippendale style, Pennsylvania or Delaware (1770-1790).

In this double chest, which stands on high ogee-bracket feet, there are three drawers in the lower section and four in the upper section, which is set within a molding (probably not original) on top of the lower. Both sections are finished with quarter columns at the corners, and applied moldings trim the tops. Dust boards separate all the drawers. While similar in style and detail, the two sections were probably not intended to be used together. The brasses are replacements. Possibly the lower section is one of the *pr. of bereaus mahogy . . . 25.00* listed in William Corbit's inventory. On the underside of the bottom board is a chalk drawing of a shield-back chair. The secondary woods are tulip and hard pine. The backboard of the upper section (a replacement) is white pine.

Dimensions: Upper section, H. 29½″ W. 35¾″ D. 19″
Lower section, H. 36⅞″ W. 44½″ D. 23½″

Owned by the heirs of Sara Corbit Levis; in the possession of Mrs. Charles Lee Reese, Jr.

TALL CLOCK, mahogany, Chippendale style, Delaware (1770-1785). [*Plate 7*]

The *clock & case in Dineing Room . . . 60.00* included in William Corbit's inventory has a scroll-top case with fluted columns flanking the face. Inset quarter columns trim the middle and lower sections of case, which rests on ogee-bracket feet. The silvered dial is engraved with broken C-scrolls at the corners, and the lunette is inscribed with the name of the clockmaker: "Duncan Beard Appoquinimink." [4] An inscription on a brass plaque on the inside of door reads: "William Corbit 1772 Clock made by Duncan Beard Clockmaker Scotchman settled one mile below Cantwells Bridge now Odessa in 1767." The secondary wood is tulip.

Dimensions: H. 105″ W. 21″ D. 10¾″

Owned by the heirs of Sara Corbit Levis; in the possession of Mrs. Charles Lee Reese, Jr.

COUCH, mahogany, Chippendale style, probably Delaware (1770-1790).

Presumably the *couch & mattrass . . . 12.00* listed in William Corbit's inventory, this unusual couch or daybed has a double chair back with interlaced pierced splat and bow-shaped cresting rail similar to side chair (Plate 5). The side rails and the straight molded legs are replacements.

Dimensions: H. 38½″ H. (rail) 17″ W. 35½″ D. 77½″

Owned by Mrs. Samuel F. Pryor III (Sara Corbit Reese).

DRESSING TABLE, mahogany, Queen Anne style, Pennsylvania or Delaware (1740-1750). [*Plate 8*]

Although dressing tables of this type are often considered to have originated in New Jersey, there is no evidence that William Corbit acquired furniture there, either by purchase or through inheritance. It is probably the *dressing table . . . 1.50* included in Corbit's inventory and is distinguished by the angular cabriole legs ending in Spanish-scroll feet. Above the double-arched skirt, four drawers are arranged in two tiers. A molded edge decorates the overhanging top. A miniature spice chest from the Sill family of Edgemont Township, Chester (now Delaware) County, shows striking similarities and suggests a Pennsylvania provenance for the dressing table.[5] An owner's stamp, "S. Higgins," on the side is presumably the mark of Sarah Corbit Higgins, granddaughter of William Corbit; there is neither family tradition nor evidence that she inherited the dressing table from her mother, Mary Clark Corbit, and it is therefore included in the list of William Corbit's furnishings. The corner brackets of the legs have been replaced. The secondary woods are white cedar and tulip.

Dimensions: H. 29⅛″ W. 33⅞″ D. 19″

Owned by the heirs of Sara Corbit Levis; in the possession of Mrs. Earle R. Crowe.

SOFA, mahogany, Federal style, Pennsylvania (1790-1800). [*Plate 9*]

Presumably the *Sopha . . . 25.00* listed in William Corbit's inventory, this transitional piece shows the influence of the neoclassical revival upon the Chippendale form. A straight back with a wide crown replaces the "camel back" of the earlier period, and straight upholstered arms frame the serpentine seat. Line inlay of satinwood embellishes the square tapered legs, which have been shortened for the addition of casters. The upholstery is modern rose brocatel, and the secondary wood is walnut. An identical sofa is owned at Wyck, the Haines house in Germantown.

Dimensions: H. 33½″ H. (seat) 14½″ W. 76″ D. 25″

Owned by the heirs of Sara Corbit Levis; in the possession of Mrs. Earle R. Crowe.

Desk and Bookcase, mahogany, Chippendale style, Pennsylvania or Delaware (1774-1790). [*Plate 10*]

The *desk and book Case . . . 30.00* listed in William Corbit's inventory has a slant-top desk section with quarter-column corners and ogee-bracket feet. The four drawers are graduated in depth. The interior of the desk is composed of a center compartment flanked by pilaster document drawers; four pigeonholes are set on either side between a single large drawer at top and two smaller drawers below. The solid door panels of the bookcase are outlined by molded ogival frames. Above the dentil cornice a broken-scroll pediment ends in carved foliage, and pierced fretwork within the pediment frames the plinth for the center finial, a basket of flowers (replacement). The secondary woods are tulip, hard pine, and white cedar.

Dimensions: H. (desk) 43¾″ W. (desk) 44½″ D. (desk) 24½″
H. (over-all) 105¼″ W. (bookcase) 40½″ D. 11¾″

Owned by the heirs of Sara Corbit Levis; in the possession of Mrs. Earle R. Crowe.

Originally willed to Pennell Corbit, this piece and the tall clock were bought in from his heirs, Mary Corbit Naudain and Sarah Corbit Higgins, by Daniel Corbit and thus descended, with the majority of the furniture listed here, through his son Daniel Wheeler Corbit to Mrs. Levis.

Looking Glass, mahogany with gilt molding, Chippendale style, Philadelphia (1770-1776.) [*Plate 11*]

Presumably the *Looking glass . . . 10.00* listed in William Corbit's inventory, this looking glass is labeled by John Elliott, a Philadelphia cabinetmaker and merchant active from 1753 until 1776.[6] The frame has a scalloped edge and is accented by a carved and gilded phoenix. The secondary woods are hemlock and larix (tamarac or larch).

Dimensions: H. 41¼″ W. 22″ D. 1″

Owned by the heirs of Sara Corbit Levis; in the possession of Mrs. Charles Lee Reese, Jr.

LOOKING GLASS, mahogany with gilt molding, Chippendale style, probably Philadelphia (1770-1785).

Presumably the *Looking glass . . . 5.00* listed in William Corbit's inventory, the elaborately scalloped frame of this looking glass has a carved and gilded phoenix within a pierced circle in the cresting. A gilt inner molding outlines the glass. An inscription in ink on the back of the frame reads: "Wm. Corbet, To be done to his order £2 12." The secondary wood is spruce.

Dimensions: H. 36″ W. 19½″ D. 1″

Owned by the heirs of Sara Corbit Levis; in the possession of Mrs. Earle R. Crowe.

CANDLESTAND, mahogany, Chippendale style, Philadelphia (1770-1785). [*Plate 12*]

Presumably the *Candle Stand 1$* included in the agreement made by Daniel Corbit and his sister Sarah Corbit Spruance in 1845, this stand features a baluster-turned shaft which rests on a tripod base with cabriole legs ending in snake's-head feet. A bird cage supports the molded-rim top.

Dimensions: H. 27⅞″ Diam. 21¾″

Owned by Mrs. D. Meredith Reese (Ann Corbit).

SHAVING STAND, mahogany, Federal style, probably Philadelphia (1810-1820). [*Plate 13*]

Presumably the *dressing Glass . . . 1.50* listed in William Corbit's inventory, the bow-front stand has three veneered drawers, the center one with an ivory escutcheon. The looking glass is mounted between turned posts, and the stand rests on turned feet. The mirror frame is veneered and inlaid, as is the framing around the drawers in the stand. The knobs are replacements. The secondary wood is white pine.

Dimensions: H. 22½″ W. 22⅛″ D. 7¾″

Owned by Mrs. Samuel F. Pryor III (Sara Corbit Reese).

BREAKFAST TABLE, mahogany, Federal style, Pennsylvania or Delaware (1800-1815). [*Plate 14*]

Presumably the *mahogany breakfast table . . . 6.00* listed in William Corbit's inventory, the table has wide drop leaves with scalloped corners. The turned-and-reeded legs end in ball feet. The knob on the single long drawer is a replacement. The secondary woods are white pine and tulip.

Dimensions: H. 28¾″ W. (closed) 21″ W. (open) 50″ D. 36″

Owned by the heirs of Sara Corbit Levis; in the possession of Mrs. Earle R. Crowe.

CARD TABLE, mahogany, Federal style, Philadelphia or Delaware (1800-1815).

Possibly the *mahogany card table . . . 5.00* listed in William Corbit's inventory, this clover-shaped table has a veneered skirt following the contour of the top. The round tapered legs are decorated with ring turnings at the top and end in turnip-shaped feet. The folding top is missing. The secondary wood is white pine.

Dimensions: H. 28½″ W. 36″ D. 17¾″

Owned by the heirs of Sara Corbit Levis; in the possession of Mrs. Earle R. Crowe.

DINING TABLE, mahogany, Federal style, Philadelphia or Delaware (1800-1820).

Presumably the *Mahogany dineing table . . . 8.00* included in William Corbit's inventory, this drop-leaf table was originally part of a two-section table. The turned-and-reeded legs with ring turnings at the top and turnip feet are often seen in Delaware and Philadelphia. The secondary wood is hard pine.

Dimensions: H. 29″ W. (closed) 20¼″ W. (open) 57¾″ D. 45″

Owned by the heirs of Sara Corbit Levis; in the possession of Mrs. Earle R. Crowe.

DINING TABLE, mahogany, Chippendale style, Philadelphia (1770-1790).

Presumably the *Mahogany dining table . . . 8.00* included in William Corbit's inventory, this drop-leaf table is rectangular in outline. The straight legs, ending in Marlborough feet, are replacements. The secondary woods are white oak and hard pine.

Dimensions: H. 28¾″ W. (closed) 19″ W. (open) 53″ D. 48″

Owned by the heirs of Sara Corbit Levis; in the possession of Mrs. Earle R. Crowe.

TEA TABLE, cherry, Chippendale style, Pennsylvania (1760-1790).

Presumably the *Round Table in Parlor . . . 4.00* included in the agreement made by Daniel Corbit and his sister Sarah Corbit Spruance in 1845, the table shows a baluster-turned shaft resting on a tripod base with cabriole legs ending in snake's-head feet. The turned supports of the bird cage repeat the turnings of the shaft. The top has a molded rim.

Dimensions: H. 28⅜″ Diam. 29½″

Owned by the heirs of Sara Corbit Levis; in the possession of Mrs. Charles Lee Reese, Jr.

Notes to Appendix I

1. Frederick B. Tolles, *Meeting House and Counting House* (Chapel Hill, North Carolina, 1948), p. 128.

2. Joshua Clayton, grandfather of John Cowgill and great-grandfather of Mary Cowgill Corbit, lived at Higham's Ferry, near Little Creek Landing in Kent County. His will, dated September 2, 1760, and probated at Dover, January 6, 1761, bequeathed a plantation and a tract of land which formed part of Higham's Ferry to his grandson John Cowgill. Two-thirds of his personal estate was to be divided equally among other of his grandchildren. This chair could have descended to Mary Cowgill Corbit and to her son Daniel Corbit, although it is not listed specifically in the notes for her will.

3. William Cox had a shop on Second Street in Philadelphia from 1767 until 1796. He is listed as a Windsor chairmaker in William M. Hornor, Jr.'s, *Blue Book Philadelphia Furniture* (Philadelphia, 1935).

4. Duncan Beard, whose shop was located on the King's Highway a mile south of Cantwell's Bridge, worked there as a clockmaker and silversmith from 1767 until his death in 1796. A Presbyterian, he served between 1770 and 1773 on the building committee for the new meeting house; and, as a Mason, he was active in Union Lodge, which was founded at Cantwell's Bridge in 1765. The secretary's jewel he made for the lodge is still in existence. About twenty tall clocks by Duncan Beard are known, two of them in the Corbit House at the present time. See Henry C. Conrad, *Duncan Beard, Clockmaker, Address Delivered at Old Drawyers Meeting House, June 3, 1928.*

5. *Antiques*, LXIX (May, 1956), 456; Letter, Bart Anderson, Chester County Historical Society, June 20, 1958.

6. Elliott's label, in both German and English, states: ". . . Looking glass [at the] Bell and Looking Glass . . . [Walnut Street] Philadelphia . . . lowest rates . . . he also new quicksilvers and frames glasses and supplies People with glass for their own Frames." The label is similar to that illustrated in Alfred Coxe Prime's "John Elliott" in *Pennsylvania Museum Bulletin*, XIX (April, 1924), and considered there to have been used by Elliott between 1768 and 1776. While Elliott's label states only that he imports and sells English looking glasses, the woods used in the frame indicate this looking glass to be of American origin.

Plate 1. Armchair, William and Mary style, probably English (1670-1710)

Plate 2. Windsor armchair, Pennsylvania (1780-1810)

Plate 3. Corner chair, Queen Anne style, probably Delaware (1740-1760)

Plate 4. Side chair, Chippendale style, Philadelphia or Delaware (1770-1790)

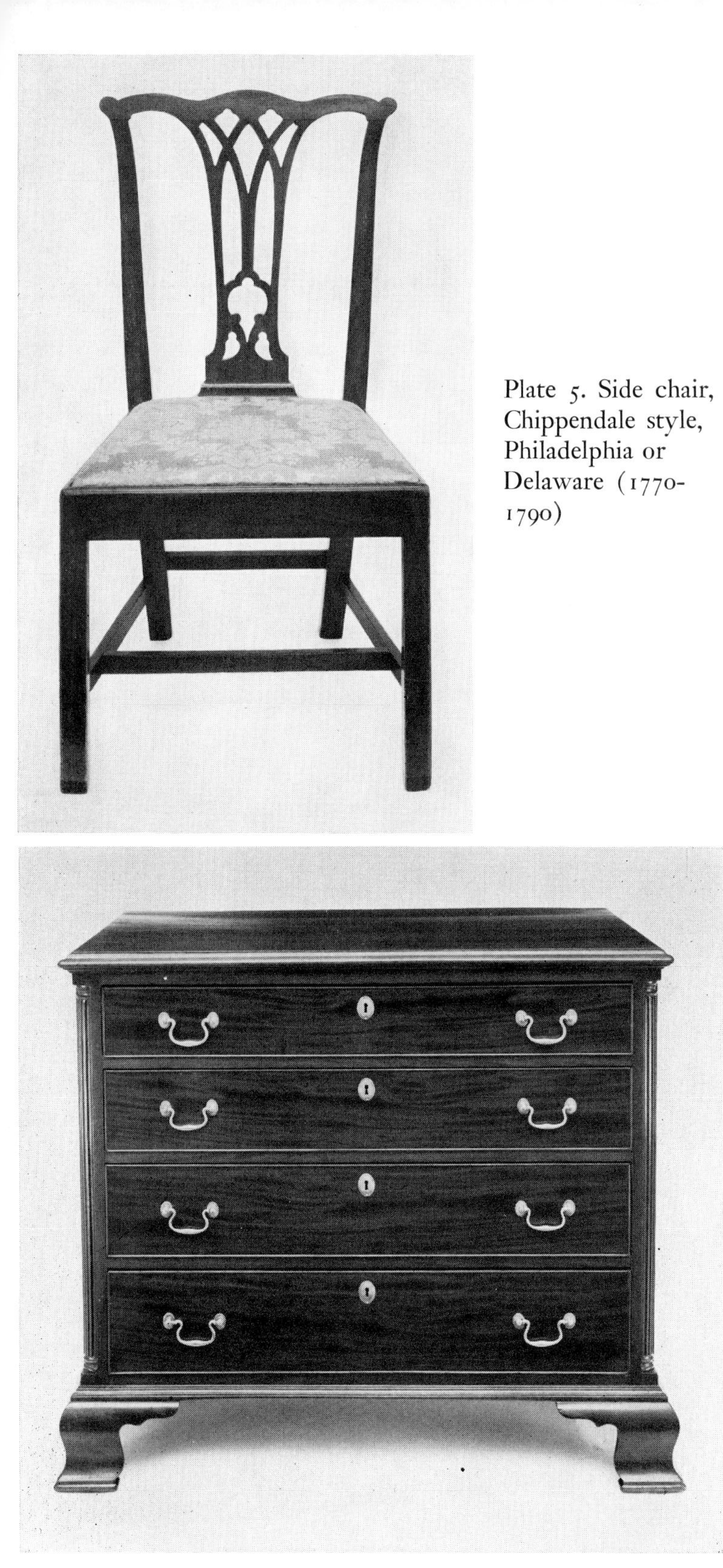

Plate 5. Side chair, Chippendale style, Philadelphia or Delaware (1770-1790)

Plate 6. Chest of drawers, Chippendale style, probably Delaware (1790-1800)

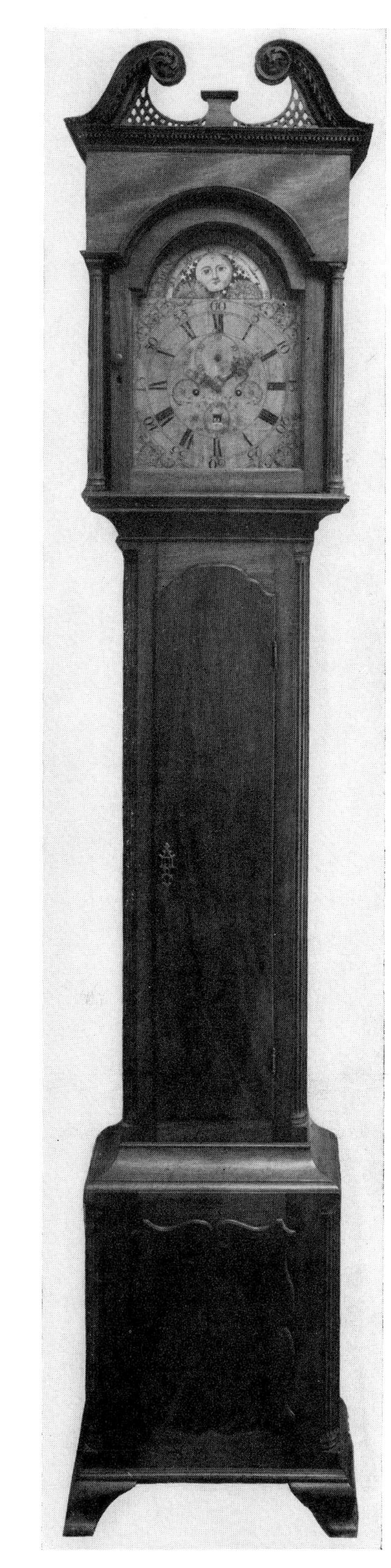

Plate 7. Tall clock, Chippendale style, Delaware (1770-1785)

Plate 8. Dressing table, Queen Anne style, Pennsylvania or Delaware (1740-1750)

Plate 9. Sofa, Federal style, Pennsylvania (1790-1800)

Plate 10. Desk and bookcase, Chippendale style, Pennsylvania or Delaware (1774-1790)

Plate 11. Looking glass, Chippendale style, Philadelphia (1770-1776)

Plate 12. Candlestand, Chippendale style, Philadelphia (1770-1785)

Plate 13. Shaving stand, Federal style, probably Philadelphia (1810-1820)

Plate 14. Breakfast table, Federal style, Pennsylvania or Delaware (1800-1815)

Appendix J

Genealogical Chart

The Ancestors and Descendants of William Corbit [1]

First Generation in America

Daniel Corbit (1682-1756) md. (possibly) Elizabeth Holdt (1688-[?])
Elizabeth England Offley (md. *c.* 1728)

Second Generation

Daniel Corbit (1715-1774) md. Mary Brinton (1708-1774)
Rachel Corbit md. Jacob Duhadaway
Ruth Corbit md. Samuel McCool
Mary Corbit md. Josiah Lewden

Third Generation

John Corbit (1740-1774) md. Lydia Aspril
Daniel Corbit (1742-1788) md. Ann Lea (1755-1789) [2]
Israel Corbit (1743-1789) md. Mary Humphries
William Corbit (1746-1818) md. Elizabeth Empson ([?]-*c.* 1770)
Mary Pennell (1749-1783)
Sarah Fisher (1758-1789)
Mary Cowgill (1761-1845)
Jonathan Corbit (1747-1777)
Mary Corbit (1749-1803) md. David Wilson (1743-1820) [3]

Fourth Generation

Children of William Corbit and Mary Pennell:

Thomas Corbit (1774-[?])
Pennell Corbit (1776-1820) md. Mary Clark (1788-1814)
Edward Corbit (1779-1795)
Thomas Corbit (1781)

Children of William Corbit and Sarah Fisher:

Mary Holliday Corbit (1785-1786)
Esther Corbit (1787)
William Fisher Corbit (1789-1827) md. Rhoda Davis

Children of William Corbit and Mary Cowgill:

John Cowgill Corbit (1792-1832) md. Harriet Trimble
Sarah Corbit (1795-1860) md. Presley Spruance (1785-1863)
Daniel Corbit (1796-1877) md. Eliza Naudain (1810-1844)
Mary Corbit Wilson (1811-1880)

Mary Corbit (1798-1826)
Thomas Corbit (1803-1821)
Rachel Thomas Corbit (1808)

FIFTH GENERATION

Children of Pennell Corbit and Mary Clark:

Sarah Clark Corbit (1810-1871) md. Anthony Madison Higgins (1809-1887)
Mary Pennell Corbit (1812-1875) md. Andrew Snow Naudain

Children of William Fisher Corbit and Rhoda Davis:

James Corbit (1814-1846)

Children of Daniel Corbit and Eliza Naudain:

John Cowgill Corbit (1834-1907) md. Emily Peterson (1837-1905)
Daniel C. Corbit (1836-1841)
Louisa A. Corbit (1838-1901) md. Charles Corbit (1838-1887) [4]
William Brinton Corbit (1840-1882) md. Virginia Love [Hellen]
Daniel Wheeler Corbit (1843-1922) md. Mary Clark Higgins (1847-1909) [5]

Children of Daniel Corbit and Mary Corbit Wilson:

Mary Corbit (1848-1923) md. Edward Tatnall Warner (1835-1904)

SIXTH GENERATION

Children of John Cowgill Corbit and Emily Peterson:

Alexander Peterson Corbit (1861-1923)
Daniel Corbit (1863-1940)
John Cowgill Corbit (1868-1906) md. Anna Gibson (1869-)

Children of Charles Corbit and Louisa A. Corbit:

Eliza Naudain Corbit (1861-1945) md. Preston Lea (1841-1916) [6]
Henry Cowgill Corbit (1863-1864)

Children of Daniel Wheeler Corbit and Mary Clark Higgins:

Sara Clark Corbit (1871-1952) md. Frederick William Curtis (1858-1911)
Charles Megarge Levis (1859-1941)
Louise Naudain Corbit (1875-1941) md. Edward L. Duer (1836-1916) [7]

Children of Edward Tatnall Warner and Mary Corbit:

Daniel Corbit Warner (1878-1895)
John Warner (1884-1911)
Edward Tatnall Warner (1889-1890)

Seventh Generation

Children of John Cowgill Corbit and Anna Gibson:

John Cowgill Corbit (1903-1904)
Ann Louise Corbit (1905-) md. David Meredith Reese (1907-)

Children of Preston Lea and Eliza Naudain Corbit:

Louise Corbit Lea (1898-) md. Paul Jennings Nowland (1895-)

Children of Frederick William Curtis and Sara Clark Corbit:

Mary Louise Curtis (1897-) md. Earle Rosman Crowe (1881-1947)
Dorothy Curtis (1900-) md. Willard Bates Purinton (1900-)
Harriet Hurd Curtis (1903-) md. Charles Lee Reese, Jr. (1903-)
Daniel Corbit Curtis (1906-1954) md. Georgia Ball [Price] (1914-)

Eighth Generation

Children of David Meredith Reese and Ann Louise Corbit:

David Meredith Reese (1935-)
John Corbit Reese (1938-)
Patricia Ann Reese (1945-)

Children of Willard Bates Purinton and Dorothy Curtis:

Anne Bates Purinton (1933-) md. Robert Parks Hazzard III
William Curtis Purinton (1936-)

Children of Charles Lee Reese, Jr., and Harriet Hurd Curtis:

Charles Lee Reese III (1928-) md. Katharine Lloyd Evans (1931-)
Peter Arnold Karthaus Reese (1932-)
Sara Corbit Reese (1932-) md. Samuel Frazier Pryor III (1928-)

Children of Daniel Corbit Curtis and Georgia Ball [*Price*]:

Mary Louise Curtis (1944-)
Alice Corbit Curtis (1946-)
Georgia Sara Curtis (1950-)
Elizabeth Brinton Curtis (1952-)

NINTH GENERATION

Children of Robert Parks Hazzard III and Ann Bates Purinton:

Robert Parks Hazzard IV (1957-)
Peter Corbit Hazzard (1958-)

Children of Charles Lee Reese III and Katharine Lloyd Evans:

Charles Lee Reese IV (1951-)
Douglas Boyd Reese (1953-)

Children of Samuel Frazier Pryor III and Sara Corbit Reese:

Samuel Frazier Pryor IV (1955-)
Katharine Lee Pryor (1957-)

Notes to Appendix J

1. This abridged genealogical chart lists the ancestors of William Corbit in America and his direct descendants closely associated with his house and the furniture contained in it. The information has been compiled from "Copy of Records (1705-1800) of Duck Creek Monthly Meeting of Friends," the Corbit family Bible in the possession of Mrs. D. Meredith Reese, and William C. Spruance's *The Spruance Family in Delaware, 1733-1933* (Wilmington, 1933). Omitted are the descendants of Presley Spruance and Sarah Corbit, Anthony Madison Higgins and Sarah Clark Corbit, and Andrew Snow Naudain and Mary Pennell Corbit; this information may be found in *The Spruance Family in Delaware.*

2. Ann Lea was the daughter of John Lea and Mary Yarnall Pennell Lea and was the half sister of William Corbit's wife, Mary Pennell.

3. David and Mary Wilson had two children: Rachel, who married Samuel Thomas, of Appoquinimink Hundred; and David, who married, first, Ann Jefferis, of Wilmington, and, second, Mary Poole, of Brandywine Village. Mary Corbit Wilson, daughter of David and Ann Wilson, married her cousin, Daniel Corbit, in 1847.

4. Charles Corbit, the son of Henry Cowgill Corbit and Sarah Bolton of Philadelphia, was the great-grandson of Daniel and Ann Lea Corbit.

5. Mary Clark Higgins was the daughter of Anthony Madison Higgins and Sarah Clark Corbit, and the great-granddaughter of William Corbit and Mary Pennell; her husband was the grandson of William Corbit and Mary Cowgill.

6. Preston Lea was the great-grandson of John Lea and Mary Yarnall Pennell Lea, the mother of Mary Pennell Corbit. His wife, through her father, the great-grandson of Daniel Corbit and Ann Lea, was the great-great-great-granddaughter of John Lea and Mary Yarnall Pennell Lea.

7. Edward L. Duer married, first, Clara Naudain, daughter of Andrew Snow Naudain and Mary Pennell Corbit.

Bibliography

PRIMARY SOURCES

The manuscript material used in this study is located in various places and is arranged in the bibliography according to location. Many of the manuscripts are privately owned, and I wish once again to express my appreciation to the Corbit descendants for permission to consult their papers.

I. MANUSCRIPTS IN PRIVATE POSSESSION

These uncatalogued papers are in four collections:

1. Papers in the possession of the heirs of Sara Corbit Levis, cited as "Corbit Papers" and now in the custody of Mrs. Levis' daughter, Mrs. Charles Lee Reese, Jr., of Wilmington.
2. Papers in the possession of Mrs. D. Meredith Reese (Ann Corbit), of Wilmington, cited as "Ann Corbit Reese Papers." The Corbit family Bible is in the possession of Mrs. Reese.
3. Papers in the possession of Mrs. Paul J. Nowland (Louise Corbit Lea), of Wilmington, cited as "Papers of Mrs. Paul J. Nowland."
4. David Wilson, "Ledger 1766-1771" is on display at the David Wilson Mansion in Odessa, as are the marriage certificates of William Corbit and Mary Pennell, February 19, 1773, and William Corbit and Mary Cowgill, April 28, 1791.

II. MANUSCRIPTS AT THE HISTORICAL SOCIETY OF DELAWARE

1. A large collection of Corbit manuscripts is contained in the "Corbit-Higgins-Spruance Papers."
2. Lewden Papers.
3. Photostatic copies of the Records of Old Drawyers Church.
4. Rodney Collection.

III. SOURCE MATERIAL AT THE HISTORICAL SOCIETY OF PENNSYLVANIA

1. "American Daily, and General Advertiser, Marriages and Death Notices, 1791-1799," *Collections of the Genealogical Society of Pennsylvania*, Vol. XLII. Philadelphia, 1899.

2. Biddle, Clement. *The Philadelphia Directory*. Philadelphia, 1791.

3. Duck Creek Monthly Meeting. "Copy of Records (1705-1800) of Duck Creek Monthly Meeting of Friends." 2 vols. MS copy (1899) of the original minutes at the Genealogical Society of Pennsylvania.

4. "A List of Marriage License Bonds So Far As Have Been Preserved in New Castle County, Delaware 1744-1836," *Collections of the Genealogical Society of Pennsylvania*, Vol. CCXLVI. Philadelphia, 1910.

5. "A List of Taxable Inhabitants residing within the County of Philadelphia, Taken Agreeably to an Act of the General Assembly . . . 1800." Manuscript Collection.

6. Logan MSS. "Quitrents of New Castle County, 1701-1713."

7. May, Robert. "Journal A, Coventry Forge: Apr. 17, 1792-August 8, 1796." Manuscript Collection.

8. May, Thomas. "Thomas May, His Waste Book, Wilmington, Dec. 12th, 1781." Manuscript Collection.

9. ———. "A Ledger Began in the Year of our Lord one Thousand Seven Hundred and Sixty two (1762)." Manuscript Collection.

10. ———."Ledger, Wilmington, 1781-1800." Manuscript Collection.

11. "Minutes of the Philadelphia Monthly Meetings." Manuscript copy of the original minutes (n.d.), at the Genealogical Society of Pennsylvania.

12. Northern District Monthly Meeting, Philadelphia. "Marriages 1772-1907, Births, Deaths, and Burials 1772-1882," *Collections of the Genealogical Society of Pennsylvania*, Vol. CDII. Philadelphia, 1921.

13. Penn MSS, Vol. XV. "Three Lower Counties on Delaware." Papers relating to administration of New Castle, Kent, and Sussex Counties.

14. "Records of Births, Marriages, and Deaths (Copied from Originals Belonging to) Society of Friends: Philadelphia Monthly Meetings 1682-1870." Manuscript copy (n.d.), at the Genealogical Society of Pennsylvania.

15. "Records of Duck Creek Monthly Meeting, 1687-1896," *Collections of the Genealogical Society of Pennsylvania*, Vol. CCXLI. Philadelphia, 1909.

16. Scully, Thomas. "Day Book, June 17, 1773." Christiana Bridge, 1773. Manuscript Collection.

17. Southern District Monthly Meeting, Philadelphia. "Births, and Burials 1772-1870, Marriages 1773-1869," *Collections of the Genealogical Society of Pennsylvania*, Vol. DXXXIX. Philadelphia, 1924.

IV. SOURCE MATERIAL AT THE CHESTER COUNTY HISTORICAL SOCIETY

1. Brinton Papers
2. Manuscript Collection

V. SOURCE MATERIAL IN THE PUBLIC ARCHIVES COMMISSION OF THE STATE OF DELAWARE

1. Kent County Wills, 1750-1800.
2. New Castle County Inventories, 1750-1825.
3. Oaths of Allegiance, Fol. 160.
4. Tax Assessment Lists: Appoquinimink, Duck Creek, St. Georges Hundreds, 1777-1783.

VI. PUBLIC RECORDS

1. Cecil County Deeds, Cecil County Court House, Elkton, Maryland.
2. Chester County Deeds, Chester County Court House, West Chester, Pennsylvania.
3. Chester County Wills, Chester County Court House, West Chester, Pennsylvania.
4. New Castle County Deeds, New Castle County Court House, Wilmington, Delaware.
5. New Castle County Wills, New Castle County Court House, Wilmington, Delaware.
6. Philadelphia County Deeds, Philadelphia County Court House, Philadelphia.

VII. SOURCE MATERIAL AT THE RIDGWAY LIBRARY, PHILADELPHIA

1. *The Charter, Laws, and Catalogue of Books, of the Library Company of Philadelphia.* [Philadelphia, 1770.]

VIII. CONTEMPORARY NEWSPAPERS

1. *Museum of Delaware* (Wilmington).
2. *Pennsylvania Chronicle* (Philadelphia).
3. *Pennsylvania Gazette* (Philadelphia).
4. *Pennsylvania Packet* (Philadelphia).
5. *Staatsbote* (Philadelphia).

SECONDARY SOURCES

ARCHITECTURE: GENERAL

Bennett, George F. *Early Architecture of Delaware.* Wilmington, 1932.

Cousins, Frank, and Riley, Phil M. *The Colonial Architecture of Philadelphia.* Boston, 1920.

Eberlein, Harold Donaldson, and Hubbard, Cortlandt Van Dyke. *Portrait of a Colonial City: Philadelphia 1670-1838.* Philadelphia, 1939.

Jackson, Joseph. *Early Philadelphia Architects and Engineers.* Philadelphia, 1923.

Jackson, *Sir* Thomas Graham. *The Renaissance of Roman Architecture.* 4 vols. Cambridge, 1921.

Kimball, Fiske. *Domestic Architecture of the American Colonies and the Early Republic.* New York, 1922.

______. "The Sources of 'Philadelphia Chippendale,' " *Pennsylvania Museum Bulletin,* XXI (June, 1926), 183-93.

Lloyd, Nathaniel. *History of the English House from Primitive Times to the Victorian Period.* 3d edition. London, 1951.

Morrison, Hugh S. *Early American Architecture, from the First Colonial Settlement to the National Period.* New York, 1952.

Peterson, Charles E. (ed.). "American Notes," *Journal of the Society of Architectural Historians,* XII (October, 1953), 28.

Pratt, Richard. *The Second Treasury of Early American Homes.* New York, 1954.

Pratt, *Sir* Roger. *The Architecture of Sir Roger Pratt.* Edited by R. T. Gunter. Oxford, 1928.

Summerson, John. *Architecture in Britain, 1530-1830.* (Pelican History of Art.) Baltimore, Maryland, 1954.

Wallace, Philip B. *Colonial Churches and Meeting Houses; Pennsylvania, New Jersey, Delaware.* New York, 1931.

Waterman, Thomas T. *The Dwellings of Colonial America.* Chapel Hill, North Carolina, 1950.

______. *The Mansions of Virginia, 1706-1776.* Chapel Hill, North Carolina, 1945.

ARCHITECTURE: DESIGN BOOKS

[Adam, Robert]. *The Works of Robert and James Adam, Esquires.* London, 1773.

Biddle, Owen. *The Young Carpenter's Assistant; or a System of Architecture, Adapted to the Style of Building in the United States.* Philadelphia, 1805.

The Builder's Dictionary: or, Gentleman and Architect's Companion. 2 vols. London, 1734.

Halfpenny, William. *The Modern Builder's Assistant.* London, 1745.

Langley, Batty. *The Builder's Directory, or Bench-Mate.* London, 1751.

Pain, William. *The Builder's Companion, and Workman's General Assistant.* London, 1758.

Palladio, Andrea. *The Four Books of Architecture.* 5 vols. Translated by Giacomo Leoni. London, 1715.

Swan, Abraham. *The British Architect: or, the Builder's Treasury of Staircases.* London, 1745.

______. *A Collection of Designs in Architecture.* 2 vols. London, 1757.

Ware, Isaac. *A Complete Body of Architecture.* London, 1756.

DELAWARE HISTORY

Conrad, Henry C. *History of the State of Delaware.* 3 vols. Wilmington, 1908.

______. *Duncan Beard, Clockmaker, Address Delivered at Old Drawyers Meeting House, June 3, 1928.*

de Valinger, Leon, Jr. "John Janvier, Delaware Cabinetmaker," *Antiques*, XLI (January, 1942), 37-39.

Federal Writers' Project of the Works Progress Administration for the State of Delaware. *Delaware, a Guide to the First State.* (American Guide Series.) New York, 1938.

Foot, George. *An Address, Embracing the Early History of Delaware, and the Settlement of Its Boundaries, and of the Drawyers Congregation . . . Delivered in Drawyers Church, Del., May 10, 1842.* Philadelphia, 1842.

Higgins, Anthony. "The Corbits on Appoquinimink, a Quaker Family of the Border South." MS in the possession of H. Rodney Sharp.

Hornor, William M., Jr. *Blue Book Philadelphia Furniture, William Penn to George Washington.* Philadelphia, 1935.

______. "James McDowell, a Delaware Cabinetmaker," *The Antiquarian*, XV (November, 1930), 64-67.

Lore, Charles B. *History of Odessa, Address at the Methodist Episcopal Church, November 18, 1901.*

Lunt, Dudley C. *The Bounds of Delaware.* Wilmington, 1947.

McCarter, J. M., and Jackson, B. F. (eds.). *Historical and Biographical Encyclopedia of Delaware.* Wilmington, 1882.

Munroe, John A. "The Philadelawareans: a Study in the Relations Between Philadelphia and Delaware in the Late Eighteenth Century," *Pennsylvania Magazine of History and Biography*, LXIX (April, 1945), 128-49.

Munroe, John A. *Federalist Delaware 1775-1815*. New Brunswick, New Jersey, 1954.

National Society of Colonial Dames of America in the State of Delaware. *A Calendar of Delaware Wills, New Castle County 1682-1800*. New York, 1911.

Reed, H. Clay (ed.). *Delaware, a History of the First State*. 3 vols. New York, 1947.

Scharf, J. Thomas. *History of Delaware 1609-1888*. 2 vols. Philadelphia, 1888.

Sweeney, John A. H. (ed.). "The Norris-Fisher Correspondence: A Circle of Friends, 1779-82," *Delaware History*, VI (March, 1955), 187-232.

Weslager, Clinton A. *Delaware's Forgotten River, the Story of the Christina*. Wilmington, 1947.

Wilmington Society of Fine Arts. *Delaware Furniture from Delaware Houses*. Catalogue of exhibition held April 5-30, 1950, Delaware Art Center, Wilmington.

Windell, Marie E. "James van Dyke Moore's Trip to the West, 1826-1828," *Delaware History*, IV (September, 1950), 69-104.

GENEALOGY

Cope, Gilbert. *Genealogy of Smedley Family*. Lancaster, Pennsylvania, 1901.

Futhey, J. Smith, and Cope, Gilbert. *History of Chester County, Pennsylvania*. Philadelphia, 1881.

Hinshaw, William Wade. *Encyclopaedia of American Quaker Genealogy*. 3 vols. Ann Arbor, Michigan, 1938.

James, Mrs. Thomas Potts. *Memorial of Thomas Potts, Junior*. Cambridge, Massachusetts, 1874.

Jordan, John W. *Colonial Families of Philadelphia*. 2 vols. New York, 1911.

Lea, James Henry, and Lea, George Henry. *The Ancestry and Posterity of John Lea*. Philadelphia, 1906.

Leach, Frank Willing. "The Brooke Family," *The North American*, Philadelphia, Sunday, October 6, 1912.

Leach, Josiah Granville. *History of the Bringhurst Family with Notes on the Clarkson, de Peyster, and Boude Families*. Philadelphia, 1901.

Schoonover, Janetta Wright. *A History of William Brinton*. Trenton, New Jersey, 1924.

Smith, Anna Wharton. *Genealogy of the Fisher Family 1682-1896*. Philadelphia, 1896.

Spruance, William C. *The Spruance Family in Delaware, 1733-1933*. Wilmington, 1933.

The William Wade Hinshaw Index to Quaker Meeting Records. Friends Historical Library, Swarthmore College.

Warner, Mary Corbit. *Brinton-Corbit Book.* Wilmington, 1907.

SOCIAL HISTORY

An Act to Incorporate the Carpenters' Company of the City and County of Philadelphia. Philadelphia, 1866.

Bishop, J. Leander. *A History of American Manufactures 1608-1860.* 2 vols. Philadelphia, 1864.

Bowden, James. *The History of the Society of Friends in America.* London, 1854.

Bridenbaugh, Carl, and Bridenbaugh, Jessica. *Rebels and Gentlemen; Philadelphia in the Age of Franklin.* New York, 1942.

Clarkson, Thomas. *A Portraiture of Quakerism.* Philadelphia, 1808.

Croker, Temple Henry; Williams, Thomas; and Clark, Samuel. *The Complete Dictionary of Arts and Sciences.* [London, 1766.]

Danckaerts, Jasper. *Journal of Jasper Danckaerts, 1679-1680.* Edited by Bartlett Burleigh James and J. Franklin Jameson. (Original Narratives of Early American History.) New York, 1952.

Depew, Chauncey M. (ed.). *1795-1895. One Hundred Years of American Commerce by One Hundred Americans.* 2 vols. New York, 1895.

Downs, Joseph. *American Furniture, Queen Anne and Chippendale Periods.* New York, 1952.

Gummere, Amelia Mott. *The Quaker, a Study in Costume.* Philadelphia, 1901.

Guthrie, William. *A New System of Modern Geography.* 2 vols. Philadelphia, 1795.

Honyman, Robert. *Colonial Panorama, 1775; Dr. Robert Honyman's Journal for March and April.* Edited by Philip Padelford. San Marino, California, 1939.

Lippincott, Horace Mather. *Early Philadelphia: Its People, Life, and Progress.* Philadelphia, 1917.

Lloyd, Arnold. *Quaker Social History.* London, 1950.

Penn, William, *Primitive Christianity Revived in the Faith and Practice of the People Called Quakers.* Wilmington, 1783.

______. *The Rise and Progress of the People Called Quakers.* Philadelphia, 1870.

Postlethwayt, Malachy. *The Universal Dictionary of Trade and Commerce.* 2 vols. [London, 1755.]

Rules of Discipline and Christian Advices of the Yearly Meeting of Friends for Pennsylvania and New Jersey. Philadelphia, 1797.

Scharf, J. Thomas, and Westcott, Thompson. *History of Philadelphia, 1609-1884.* Philadelphia, 1884.

Tolles, Frederick B. *George Logan of Philadelphia.* New York, 1953.
______. *Meeting House and Counting House, the Quaker Merchants of Colonial Philadelphia, 1682-1763.* Chapel Hill, North Carolina, 1948.
Watson, John F. *Annals of Philadelphia, and Pennsylvania, in the Olden Time, Being a Collection of Memoirs, Anecdotes, and Incidents of the City and Its Inhabitants.* 3 vols. Philadelphia, 1927.

BIBLIOGRAPHICAL SOURCES

British Museum. *Catalogue of Printed Books, 1881-1900.* Ann Arbor, Michigan, 1946.
Sabin, Joseph; Eames, Wilberforce; and Vail, R. W. G. *Bibliotheca Americana. A Dictionary of Books Relating to America, from Its Discovery to the Present Time.* New York, 1868-1936.
Union Library Catalog at University of Pennsylvania.
U. S. Library of Congress. *A Catalog of Books Represented by Library of Congress Printed Cards.* Ann Arbor, Michigan, 1942-1946; 1942-1947; 1948-1952.

Index

Adam, Robert, 47
Alexander, Joseph, 23, 75, 97
Allegiance, oath of, *see* Corbit, William (1746-1818), allegiance to Delaware
Allfree, William, 24
Andros, Sir Edmund (Gov. of Colony of New York), 4
Annapolis, Md., 5
Appoquinimink (first name for Odessa), *see* Odessa
Appoquinimink Bridge, *see* Odessa
Appoquinimink Creek, 4
  see also Odessa, commercial growth of
Appoquinimink Hundred, Del., 6, 22, 23, 48, 76
Architects, *see* Adam, Robert; Biddle, Owen; Corbit House, architect of; May, Robert
Architectural details, contemporary names of, 46-47
  Delaware shutters and blinds, 42
  doors, "Philadelphia-style," 42
  walls (painted), expense of, 45
  see also Christ Church, Philadelphia; Corbit House, architectural details; Powel, Samuel, House, Philadelphia; Stamper-Blackwell House, Philadelphia
Architecture, construction process, 18th century, 69-70
  Delaware regional form, 3, 61-62
  French mode, 52
  "Quaker plan," 61
  see also British Architect; Builder's Dictionary; Designs in Architecture; Kent Co.; Maryland; New Castle; New Castle Co.; Odessa; Philadelphia; "The Sources of 'Philadelphia Chippendale' "; Wilmington
Aspendale, Downs Chapel, 61

Baker, Jacob, 29
Beard, Duncan, 43, 110, 114, 119
Bedford, Gunning, 47
Benson, Hilent, 94
Benson, Jannet, 94
Bettle, Ann (Brinton), 15, 16, 17
Bettle, Samuel, 15, 16, 17
Bettle, Sarah (Beakes), 17
Bettle, William, 17-18, 19
Biddle, Owen, 29
Birmingham Township, Pa., 15-16
  see also Friends, Society of, Meeting House, Birmingham
Bishop, J. Leander, 19
Bohemia Manor, 4, 5, 6
Bohemia River, 5
Brandywine Creek, flour mills, 5-6
  Lea mills, 22
Bridges, *see* Odessa, toll bridge and house
Bringhurst, James, 45, 71, 84
Brinton, Jane, 15
Brinton, William, 15
Brinton, William (first), 15
Brinton family, 15
Brinton's Mill, Concord, Pa., 15
Brinton-Corbit Book, Mary Corbit Warner, 15
British Architect, The, Abraham Swan, 52, 56
Brooke, John, 49
Brunor, George, 28
Bryans, John, 44, 81, 82
Builder's Dictionary, The, 46

Cabinetmakers, *see* Douglass, John; Elliott, John; Janvier, John
Cain, Miles, 57

Cantwell, Edmund (Capt.), 4
Cantwell, Richard, 4
Cantwell Mutual Fire Insurance Company, 77
Cantwell's Bridge (second name for Odessa), *see* Odessa
Carpenters' Company, Philadelphia, 48, 52
Chairmakers, *see* Cox, William
Chesapeake Bay, 5
Chester, Pa., 44, 81, 84
Chester County, Pa., 8, 13, 23
Christ Church, Philadelphia, 56
Christiana, Del., 5, 6, 60
see also Lewden, John, House, Christiana
Christiana Bridge, *see* Christiana, Del.
Christina Creek, 16
Churches and congregations, *see* Christ Church, Philadelphia; Friends, Society of; Old Drawyers Presbyterian Church, Odessa; Presbyterians; St. Anne's Church, Middletown, Del.
Clark, John, 75
Clayton, Joshua, 111, 119
"Clio" steamer, 78
Cliveden, 71
Clockmakers, *see* Beard, Duncan
Colleges and universities, *see* Haverford College; University of Delaware
Colonies, technical independence of, on eve of the Revolution, 69
Continental currency, 23
Cook, John, 75
Corbet, William, 15
Corbit, Alexander Peterson (1861-1923), 31, 126
Corbit, Ann (Lea) (1755-1789), 29, 32, 125
Corbit, Daniel (1682-1756), 13-14, 76, 125
Corbit, Daniel (1715-1774), 13-16, 125
Corbit, Daniel (1742-1788), 13, 16, 29, 32, 125
Corbit, Daniel (1796-1877), 20, 25, 30, 75, 76-77, 97, 100, 101, 110, 112, 113, 116, 117, 126
Corbit, Daniel (1863-1940), 31, 126
Corbit, Daniel Wheeler (1843-1922), 77-78, 110, 116, 126, 127
Corbit, Edward (1779-1795), 23, 27, 125
Corbit, Eliza (Naudain) (1810-1844), 76, 100, 126
Corbit, Elizabeth (Empson) (?-*c.* 1770), 20, 125
Corbit, Elizabeth (England) [Offley] (md. *c.* 1728), 14, 125
Corbit, Elizabeth (Holdt) (1688-?), 14, 125
Corbit, Israel (1743-1789), 14, 16-17, 29, 32, 125
Corbit, James (1814-1846), 100, 126
Corbit, John (1740-1774), 23, 125
Corbit, John Cowgill (1792-1832), 25, 27, 30, 75, 96, 126
Corbit, John Cowgill (1834-1907), 31, 126
Corbit, John Cowgill (1868-1906), 110, 126, 127
Corbit, Joseph, 31
Corbit, Mary (1798-1826), 25, 30, 75, 98, 126
Corbit, Mary (Brinton) (1708-1774), 14-16, 125
Corbit, Mary (Clark), 75, 115, 125, 126
Corbit, Mary Clark (Higgins) (1847-1909), 77, 126, 127
Corbit, Mary (Wilson) (1811-1880), 77, 126
Corbit, Mary (Cowgill) (1761-1845), 25, 30, 75, 96, 111, 125, 126
Documents, Minutes for the will of, 100
Corbit, Mary (Humphries), 14, 32, 125
Corbit, Mary (Pennell) (1749-1783), 22-24, 30, 45, 69, 125, 126
Illus., marriage certificate of William Corbit and Mary Pennell, 21
Corbit, Pennell (1776-1820), 23, 25-28, 75, 76, 77, 96, 97, 98, 99, 116, 125, 126
Corbit, Rachel Thomas (1808), 25, 126
Corbit, Rhoda (Davis), 76, 126
Corbit, Sarah (Fisher) (1758-1789), 24-25, 125, 126
Corbit, Thomas (1774-?), 23, 30, 125
Corbit, Thomas (1781), 23, 125
Corbit, Thomas (1803-1821), 25, 75, 97, 98, 126
Corbit, William (1746-1818), 4, 8, 22-23, 39, 43, 49 110-118, 125-126
allegiance to Delaware (1778), 23-24
apprenticeship, 17
biography, 8-9, 13, 29-30
books, attitude toward, 26-27
children of, 22-23, 25, 125-126
Continental currency, 23

Corbit, William (*cont.*)
death of, 30
education, attitude toward, 26-27
farms of, 23, 27, 28-29
finances of, 28-29
letters of, 26-27
library of, 30, 104-109
marriages of, 20, 22, 24-25, 69, 75, 125
Passyunk Twp., Pa., 27-28
personality of, 9, 18, 20, 22, 39, 44, 70-71
Philadelphia, contact with and influence on him, 8-9, 17-18, 24, 27, 28, 39, 50, 52, 71, 110
political life, 30
Quaker, as a, 20, 22, 23-25, 50, 57, 70-71
slave owner, 20, 22, 24, 28
tannery, 4, 8-9, 18-20, 23, 25-29, 75, 76, 96, 98
war, opposition to, 23
will of, 25, 96-99
Documents, 69-70; Will of William Corbit, 96-99
Illus., marriage certificate of William Corbit and Mary Pennell, 21
see also Corbit House, Odessa
Corbit, William Fisher (1789-1827), 25, 27, 75, 76, 97, 99, 126
Corbit family, 15, 16, 75-76
genealogical chart of, 125-128
papers collected, 77
Corbit House, Odessa, architect of, 48, 49, 52, 57
architectural details, exterior, 42, 46-47, 52, 56; interior, 42-44, 46-47, 50, 52, 56-57
architectural importance of, 79
comparison of, 39, 49-50, 52, 57, 60, 70-71
construction of, 22, 44-48, 69-70
cost of, 44-47
description of, exterior, 22, 42, 45, 49-50, 61; interior, 42-44
design of, 52, 56-57, 110
drawing room ("long room"), 43-44, 50, 56-57, 70
furnishings of, 28, 43, 70-71, 77-79, 110-119
heating of, 43
land for, 39
library, 77
modernizations of, 78
paneling of, 46, 60, 61-62
Corbit House, Odessa (*cont.*)
restoration of, 78-79
start of (1772), 22, 39
symbol of, 9, 71, 79
vacant, 28
views from, 4, 43, 44
workmen on, 45-46, 47-48, 56-57, 71
Documents, 69-70; Bill of Robert May and Company, 86-93; Deed for the Corbit House site, 94-95; Inventory of William Corbit's estate, 102-105; William Corbit's building accounts, 81-85
Illus., architectural details, 53; exterior, 2, 7; floor plan, 41; furniture, 120, 121, 122, 123, 124; interior, frontispiece, 12, 40, 51; land survey, 38
see also Corbit, Daniel (1796-1877); Corbit, Mary (Cowgill) (1761-1845); Corbit, Pennell (1776-1820); Corbit, William (1746-1818); Winterthur Museum; Sharp, H. Rodney
Corbit Library, Odessa, 3, 57
Cowgill, John, 25, 119
Cowgill, Joseph, 29
Cox, William, 119
Craftsmen, 46, 56-57, 70
see also Cabinetmakers; Chairmakers; Clockmakers; Corbit House, workmen
Creeks, *see* Rivers and creeks
Cresson, James, 63
Cresson, Jeremiah, 64, 82
Crowe, Mary Louise (Curtis) (Mrs. Earle R.) (1897-), 110, 112, 113, 114, 115, 116, 117, 118, 127
Curry, Jasper, 97
Currying, 19
Curtis, Daniel Corbit (1906-1954), 110, 127, 128
Curtis, Sara Clark (Corbit) (Mrs. Frederick William), 127
see also Levis, Sara Clark (Corbit) [Curtis]

Dale, Richard C., 97, 98
Danckaerts, Jasper, journal of, 4, 5
de Hinijossa, Alexander, 4
Delany, Margaret (Robinson), 8
Delany, Sharp, 8
Delaware, politics, 30, 75-76

Delaware College, *see* University of Delaware
Delaware Railroad, 77-78
Delaware River, 5-6
Deschler House, Germantown, Pa., 49
Designs in Architecture, Abraham Swan, 52, 56
Illus., 54, 55
Dickinson, John, 33
Dickinson, Mary (Norris), 22, 24
Dickson and Millins, 45, 84
Directories, see *Philadelphia Directory* (for 1791)
Dorsey, Abraham, 96
Douglass, John, 36
Dover, Del., 5, 8, 61-62
see also Hillyard-Cowgill House, Dover
Drawyers Creek, 22, 61
Drinker, Daniel, 28-29
Duck Creek, 6, 24
see also Friends, Society of, Monthly Meeting, Duck Creek
Duer, Louise (Corbit) (1875-1941), 78, 127
Duhadaway, Jacob, 14, 125
Duhadaway, Rachel (Corbit), 14, 125
du Pont, Henry Francis, Winterthur Museum, *see* Winterthur Museum

Elk Forge, Md., 48-49
Elk River, 49
Elkton, Maryland, 49
Elliott, John, 110, 116, 119
Empson, Cornelius, 20
Empson, Cornelius (justice of peace), 20
Empson, Mary, 20
Empson, Sarah (Wilson), 20
Epidemics, Philadelphia (1799), 27

Farming, 3, 5-6
see also Orchards, peach
Federal Republicans, 30
Federalist Party, 30
Fisher, Fenwick, 24, 76
Fisher, Joshua, 76
Fisher, Mary (Holliday), 24
Fisher, Miers, 36
Flour, superfine, 5
Floyd, Samuel, 44, 57
Folwell, John, 56
Free Masons, Union Lodge, Odessa, 119
Friends Boarding School, Westtown, Pa., 30
Friends School, Smyrna, Del., 76
Friends, Society of, Meeting House, Birmingham, 14
Meeting House, Little Creek, 25
Meeting House, Odessa, 3, 30
Monthly Meeting, Duck Creek, 13, 14, 20, 24
Monthly Meeting, Wilmington, 24
politics, attitude toward, 30
Preparative Meeting, Georges Creek, 13, 16, 20, 22
Yearly Meeting, Philadelphia, 8, 15, 20
see also Corbit, William (1746-1818), as a Quaker; Friends Boarding School, Westtown, Pa.; Friends School, Smyrna, Del.

Genealogies, *see Brinton-Corbit Book;* Corbit family, genealogical chart of
Grant, John, 13
Gray's Ferry, Pa., 27
Greene, Mrs. Howard, 60
Guthrie, William, 6

Hagg, Mary C., 100
Hanson, Joseph, 48
Harbors and ports, *see* Odessa, port in; Philadelphia, collector of customs
see also Transportation, water; Travel
Haverford College, 77
Hayes, John, 49
see also May, Robert, and Company
Hayes, Stephen, 49
see also May, Robert, and Company
Head of Elk, Md., 5, 49, 60
see also Partridge Hill, Head of Elk; Rudolph, Tobias, House, Head of Elk
"Herman's cartroad," 5
Higgins, Sarah Clark (Corbit) (1810-1871), 100, 115, 116, 126, 129
Higham's Ferry, Kent Co., 119
Hillyard-Cowgill House, Dover, 61
Historic houses, *see* Aspendale, Downs Chapel; Cliveden; Corbit House, Odessa; Wilson, David, Mansion, Odessa; Deschler House, Germantown; Hillyard-Cowgill House, Dover; Moore, James, House; Lewden, John, House, Christiana; Johns,

Historic houses (*cont.*)
Kensey, House, New Castle; Lackford Hall; Mount Pleasant; Partridge Hill, Head of Elk; Powel, Samuel, House, Philadelphia; 1704 House; Stamper-Blackwell House, Philadelphia; Rudolph, Tobias, House, Head of Elk; Woodford
Historical Society of Delaware, Corbit-Higgins-Spruance Papers, 44
History of Delaware 1609-1888, J. Thomas Scharf, 13, 23
Honyman, Robert (Dr.), 3
Hoodt, Casper, 14

Iron manufacture, *see* Elk Forge, Maryland; Stedman, Charles

Janvier, John, 30, 105, 110, 114
Jefferson, Thomas, 30
Johns, Kensey, House, New Castle, 61-62
Jones, Cantwell, 29-30
Jones, John, 22

Kelly, George F., 57
Kent Co., Del. 61
Kimball, Fiske, 52
King's Highway (King's Road), 5, 23

Labadists (Dutch), 4
Lackford Hall, 61
Lafever, Samuel, 57
Lea, John, 22
Lea mills, *see* Brandywine Creek
Levis, Sara Clark (Corbit) [Curtis] (1871-1952), 78, 110, 127
Lewden, John, 60
Lewden, Josiah, 14, 125
Lewden, Mary (Corbit), 14, 125
Lewden, Rachel, 14
Lewden family, 60
Lewden, John, House, Christiana, 60-61
Illus., 59
Libraries, *see* Carpenters' Company, Philadelphia; Corbit, William (1746-1818), library of; Corbit Library, Odessa; Jones, Cantwell; Library Company of Philadelphia
see also Philadelphia, bookstore
Library Company of Philadelphia, 18, 52
Lippincot, Richard, 45, 84
Liston, William, 98
Little Creek, Del., 6
see also Friends, Society of, Meeting House, Little Creek
Logan, Deborah (Norris), 24
Lovelace, Francis (Gov.), 13
Lower Counties, 8
see also Kent County; New Castle County; Philadelphia, influence of

Macoole, John, 13
Macoole, Mary (Howie), 13
MacPherson, Jack, 33
Martin, Abraham, 4
Martin, Edward, 23
Maryland, 5, 6
architecture, 3
Masonic Order, *see* Free Masons, Union Lodge, Odessa
May, Elizabeth (Brooke), 49
May, Frances, 48
May, Rebecca (Potts), 52
May, Robert, 49
May, Robert (1750-?), 46-50, 56, 60-61, 69
see also Corbit House, architect of; May, Robert, and Company
May, Robert, and Company, 45-49, 57, 60
bill to William Corbit, 45-47, 69-70, 78, 86-93
Illus., bill from, 68
May, Thomas (?-1792), 48-49
McCool, John, 14
McCool, Ruth (Corbit), 14, 125
McCool, Samuel, 14, 125
M'Culloh, Anna, 36
Merchants, *see* Bringhurst, James; Corbit, Daniel (1796-1877); Corbit, William Fisher (1789-1827); Drinker, Daniel; Elliott, John; Fisher, Fenwick; Hayes, John; Hayes, Stephen; May, Thomas (?-1792); Seal, Joshua; Wharton, Joseph; Wilson, David (1743-1820); Wilson, Edward
Meriss, Benjamin, 29
Meriss, John, 29
"Middle Neck," 13-14
Middletown, Del., 5, 77-78
see also St. Anne's Church, Middletown
Mills and milling, *see* Brandywine Creek; Drawyers Creek
Moore, James, 23

Moore, Prudence, 23
Moore, James, House, 57, 60-61
Illus., 59
Moreton, Robert, 13
Morse, Louisa (Spruance) (Mrs. Albert W., Jr.), 113
Mount Pleasant, 49, 71
Murry, Alice, 25, 99
Museums, *see* Philadelphia Museum of Art; Winterthur Museum

Naudain, Elias, 76
Naudain, Mary Pennell (Corbit) (1812-1875), 100, 116, 126
New Amstel, *see* New Castle
New Castle, Del., 4
architecture, 61-62
see also Architectural details, Delaware shutters and blinds; Kensey Johns House, New Castle
New Castle County, Del., architecture, 3, 61
sheriff of, 4
tanneries, 17
see also Farming
New Castle County National Bank, 77
New System of Husbandry (A), 49
Newport, Del., 6
Newspapers, *see Pennsylvania Chronicle; Pennsylvania Gazette; Pennsylvania Packet; Philadelphia Gazette*
Noble, Samuel, 18
Northern Liberties, Pa., 17, 29
Nowland, Louise Corbit (Lea) (Mrs. Paul J.), 114, 127

Odessa, Del., 19, 22, 27, 28, 75, 94
architecture, 3 [60
commercial growth, 4-6, 16, 29, 49-50,
decline of, 77-78
description of (1679), 4
history of, 4-5
names of, 3, 77
Philadelphia, influence on, 6, 8-9, 16, 49, 71
port in, 5, 69
toll bridge and house, 4-5
transportation center, 5-6
travel from and to, 5-6, 8
see also Corbit House; Wilson, David, Mansion; Friends, Society of, Meeting House, Odessa; Moore, James, House; Old Drawyers Presbyterian Church
"Odessa Days," 79
Odessa Loan Association, 77
Offley, Caleb, 14
Offley, Caleb (younger), 14
Offley, David, 14
Offley, Michael, 14
Old Drawyers Presbyterian Church, Odessa, 3, 5, 44-45, 57, 60-61, 77
Illus., 74
Orchards, peach, 76

Partridge Hill, Head of Elk, 60-61
Passyunk Twp., Pa., 27-28
Pegg's Run, Northern Liberties, 17
Penington, Samuel, 105
Penn, William, 4
Pennell, Thomas, 22
Pennsylvania Chronicle, 17-18
Pennsylvania Gazette, 18
Pennsylvania Packet, 64
Perkenpine, John, 29
Philadelawarean, 8
Philadelphia, 13, 49, 50
architecture, 9, 28, 39, 43, 70-71, 110
bookstore, 52
collector of customs, 8
commerce of, 6, 8
communication with, 5
influence of, 6, 8, 16, 49, 71
tanners and tanneries, 17, 18-19, 39
see also Carpenters' Company, Philadelphia; Christ Church, Philadelphia; Deschler House, Germantown; Epidemics, Philadelphia, 1799; Friends, Society of, Yearly Meeting, Philadelphia; Library Company of Philadelphia; Philadelphia Museum of Art; Powel, Samuel, House, Philadelphia; Stamper-Blackwell House, Philadelphia; Wetherill and Cresson
Philadelphia Directory (1791), 26
Philadelphia Gazette, 49
Philadelphia Museum of Art, Powel, Samuel, House, drawing room, 50
Physicians, *see* Honyman, Robert (Dr.)
Politics, *see* Corbit, William (1746-1818), political life; Delaware, politics; Federal Republicans; Federalist Party;

Politics (*cont.*)
Friends, Society of, politics, attitude toward
Potts, Joseph, 52
Powel, Samuel, 52
Powel, Samuel, House, Philadelphia, 47, 49-50, 56, 71
Illus., 51, 53
Presbyterians, 5
see also Old Drawyers Presbyterian Church, Odessa
Preston, Jonas (?-1773), 22, 29 [22
Preston, Mary (Yarnall) [Pennell] [Lea],
Pryor, Sara Corbit (Reese) (Mrs. Samuel Frazier, III) (1932-), 110, 113, 115, 117, 127, 128
Purinton, Dorothy (Curtis) (Mrs. Willard B.) (1900-), 110, 127

"Quaker Martyr," *see* Cowgill, John
"Quaker plan," *see* Architecture, Quaker
Quakers, *see* Friends, Society of
Quercus falcata, see Tanning, Spanish-oak bark

Reading, Philip, 39, 42
Illus., survey of Corbit property, 38
Red Lion, Del., 5, 76
Reese, Ann Louise (Corbit) (Mrs. D. Meredith) (1905-), 31, 110, 111, 112, 117, 127
Reese, Harriet (Curtis) (Mrs. Charles Lee, Jr.) (1903-), 110, 111, 112, 114, 115, 116, 118, 127, 128
Revolutionary War, 23
see also Corbit, William (1746-1818), war, opposition to
Reynolds, Th. P., 105
Richards, Daniel, 26
Richards, Rachel (Bettle), 27
Ridley Creek, 22
Rivers and creeks, *see* Appoquinimink Creek; Bohemia River; Brandywine Creek; Delaware River; Drawyers Creek; Elk River; Ridley Creek; Sassafras River; Schuylkill River
Rivington, James, 52
Roads, *see* Transportation, roads
Robinson, Thomas, 11
Rodney, Caesar A., 30 [61
Rudolph, Tobias, House, Head of Elk, 60-

St. Anne's Church, Middletown, 42
St. Georges Hundred, Del., 6, 22, 76, 94
Sassafras River, 5
Scattergood, Thomas, 26
Scharf, J. Thomas, 13, 23, 60, 61
Schlosser, George, 18
Schools, *see* Friends Boarding School, Westtown; Friends School, Smyrna
Schuylkill River, 9, 27, 28
Seal, Joshua, 49
see also May, Robert, and Company
Sellers, Nicholas, 44, 81, 82
1704 House, 15
Sharp, H. Rodney, 78, 79, 114
Shriver, Henry, 29
Society of Friends, *see* Friends, Society of
"Sources of 'Philadelphia Chippendale,'" Fiske Kimball, 52
South River, *see* Delaware River
Spanish-oak bark, *see* Tanning, Spanish-oak bark
Sperger, Martin Kocker, 28
Spring Garden, Philadelphia, 29
Spruance, Alice (Lea) (Mrs. William C.), 113
Spruance, Presley (1785-1863), 30, 76, 126
Spruance, Sarah (Corbit) (1795-1860), 25, 30, 75, 76, 77, 98, 100, 101, 110, 113, 117, 126
Spruance, William Corbit, 110
Stagecoach, *see* Travel
Stamper, John, 50
Stamper-Blackwell House, Philadelphia, 42, 50
Starr, Isaac, 44, 83
Starr, John, 96, 98, 99
Starr, Thomas, 28, 44, 85
Stedman, Ann (Graeme), 50
Stedman, Charles, 50, 52
Stride, Joseph, 45, 84, 85
Swan, Abraham, 52, 56

Tanners and tanneries, *see* Bettle, William; Brunor, George; Corbit, Daniel (1796-1877); Corbit, Pennell (1776-1820); Corbit, William (1746-1818), tannery; Lewden, John; New Castle Co.; Noble, Samuel; Philadelphia; Scattergood, Thomas; Schlosser, George; Wilmington
see also Tanning

Tanning, equipment for, 18-19
ingredients in, 18-19
market for, 27, 28
process of, 19-20, 28
profit from, 18, 20
Spanish-oak bark, 18, 23, 76
see also Tanners and tanneries
Tatman, Charles, 76
Tatman, Harriet Brinton (Trimble) [Corbit], 76, 100, 126
Thomas, Evan, 99
Thomas, Samuel, 97, 98
Tilton, Nehemiah, 30
Tolls, *see* Odessa, toll bridge and house
Transportation, 6
roads, 5, 23, 60
water, 5, 69, 77-78
see also Travel
Travel, 5, 6, 8
stagecoach, 8
see also Transportation

University of Delaware, ix, 77, 79
see also Winterthur Museum

Van Dyke, Abraham, 44, 83
Van Dyke, David, 44, 82, 83
Varlo, John, 49

Walker, William, 44, 83
Waterman, Thomas, 42
West Indies, 5
Wetherill and Cresson, Philadelphia, 44, 63, 81
Wetherill and sons, 63
Wharton, Joseph, 71
Wilmington, Del., 5, 8, 16, 48-49
Wilmington, Del. (*cont.*)
architecture, 61
tanners and tanneries, 76
see also Friends, Society of, Monthly Meeting, Wilmington
Wilson, David (1743-1820), 6, 16, 20, 22, 29, 39, 45, 77, 84, 85, 98, 99, 125
ledger of, 6, 18, 48, 57
Documents, Deed for the Corbit House site, 94-95
see also Wilson, David, Mansion, Odessa
Wilson, Edward, 36
Wilson, James, 57
Wilson, Jonathan, 48
Wilson, Margaret (Empson) (?-1768), 20
Wilson, Mary (Corbit) (1749-1803), 20, 22, 32, 77, 125
Wilson, David, Mansion, Odessa, 3, 43, 44, 57, 60-61
Illus., 58
see also Corbit Library, Odessa; Wilson, David (1743-1820)
Winterthur Corporation, *see* Winterthur Museum
Winterthur Museum (The Henry Francis du Pont Winterthur Museum), Corbit House, 79
Stamper-Blackwell House, parlor, 50
Winterthur Program in Early American Culture, ix-x, 79
Woodburn, *see* Hillyard-Cowgill House, Dover
Woodford, 49
Woolly, Edmund, 17

Young, Samuel, 44, 84

Zantzinger, Adam, 28